Concentration

Maintain Laser Sharp Focus & Attention for Stretches of 5 Hours or More

Kam Knight

Visit MindLily.com/ir for your free gift:

Conquer Your Internal Resistance to Make More Money, Have Better Relationships, and Live a Fulfilling Life

Download today as it may not be available tomorrow

Copyright © 2019
All rights Reserved.

Table of Contents

SECTION I -
INTRODUCTION TO
CONCENTRATION

INTRODUCTION

As humans, we like to think of ourselves as these walking, talking, thinking, wholly conscious beings. We assume that anything we do—be it exercising, having a conversation, or solving a problem—is simply a matter of *just doing it*.

We often forget, however, that extremely complex, intricate, and sophisticated processes inside the mind and body allow us to do what we do. For example, when watching TV, the eyes receive millions of light rays from the screen to form an image. Based on that image, the brain floods the body with feelings of joy, fear, laughter, or any other emotion the show is trying to convey.

In the same way, a complex reaction occurs with something as simple as moving your hand. First, the brain sends signals to nerve cells in the spinal cord called *motor neurons*. Each motor neuron is connected to a specific muscle group, such as the bicep, quadricep, or forearm. When a motor neuron fires, impulses travel to those muscles, releasing a chemical that causes them to relax or contract.

Of course, we don't think about any of this when moving our hands. We're not saying to ourselves *I'd like to fire my motor neurons just enough so the muscle fibers in the fingers contract by two inches and relax in the forearms by three inches.* Nope! We only think, *I'd like to take a bite of this apple,* and it just happens. In fact, we may not even think that. Simply seeing the apple activates the complex process to automatically pick it up and put it in our mouth.

These are just two examples of the thousands of processes inside the mind and body. Another example is the way the ears convert vibrations in the air to recognize sound or how the vocal cords create similar vibrations to form words. Then, of course, there are our thoughts, feelings, drives, impulses, memories, habits, and let's not forget the digestive system, which converts food into energy to give these processes the fuel to function.

2

As you can see, humans are made up of a complex set of mechanisms, chemical reactions, and processes. These reactions and processes are so fast and fluid, we don't notice them take place. In fact, we don't even notice they exist.

Even more, many of these processes are outside our conscious control. We believe we're in control or directing our decisions and actions, but in truth, they are running the show.

If this is difficult to accept, think about the last time you saw someone so attractive, you couldn't keep your eyes off him or her. You may have thought that you chose to fix your eyes on that person, but technically, it wasn't you. It was one of the mechanisms built to find an attractive mate.

The attraction mechanism took over and placed your eyes on the individual, then pushed a series of arousing emotions so you couldn't help but keep them there. And if the emotions were strong enough, you were likely willing to *pay attention* to anything this person said or did.

Again, this feeling of arousal happened on its own, without any conscious decision or choice—and before you could even think about it. For one reason or another, the attraction mechanism found this particular person appealing.

If, however, she says or does something that your mechanism doesn't like, attention would vanish as instantly as it arose, leaving you unable to engage with him or her even if you tried. Your attention was there because one of your processes wanted it there, and the attention left because that same process *changed its mind*.

Much like attraction, our thoughts, decisions, and actions are too operating on their own. Believe it or not, many of the thoughts we think and the decisions we make, as well as the actions that we take to carry out those decisions, happen outside of our conscious awareness and control.

If this too is difficult to accept, think back to a time when you said something and then asked yourself, *Why the heck did I just say that?* Especially when you intended to say something entirely different. I would suggest that you didn't say it, a process within your unconscious did.

3

Or, have you ever wanted to do something really bad, but for the life of you, couldn't? As a result, you began thinking that there was something wrong with you. Well, one or more of your inner mechanisms, likely the defense mechanism, held you back or got in the way.

Our internal mechanisms have the ability to take control of our decisions and actions, and convince us to do things or to not do them. In fact, these mechanisms not only take control, they are the very process by which decisions and actions are made.

In other words, it's through our mechanisms that we are able to make decisions and take action, and if those mechanisms decide to get in the way, they very well can—and they very well do. There are many reasons why they do, which you'll uncover in this book.

The point is, you are a collection of intricate and complex mechanisms, many of which are outside your conscious awareness. More importantly, these mechanisms are influencing countless aspects of your life, including your ability to concentrate.

To improve concentration, it's important, therefore, to understand both the mechanisms that create focus and those that distract and take them away. Understanding how these mechanisms work, what drives them, and how they influence your thoughts, feelings, and behaviors is the key to enhancing this ability.

It's important to understand, you can't merely *will* yourself to make changes or improvements. Unfortunately, the mind and body don't work that way. Think about how difficult it is to lose weight. It is so difficult because there are numerous mechanisms designed to stop you.

One such mechanism is habit. Habits are designed to keep you in a specific routine or pattern of behavior. No matter what other options exist, habits will do everything they can to bring you back to that specific routine or pattern. This is what they are built to do.

Therefore, anytime you attempt to eat healthy or to exercise, the habit will find all sorts of ways to block those attempts. Even if the habit is no longer useful, enjoyable, or downright harmful to your health, it will persist to

4

keep you in it. If habits didn't, they wouldn't be very good at what they did now would they?

If you approached weight loss like most people, believing that eating better or exercising was simply a matter of choosing to eat better and exercise, you'd be in for a rude awakening. The first few days might go well, but once the old habits kicked in, tremendous resistance, difficulty, and pain would arise.

Like most people, you would quickly give up. The internal mechanisms would win, and you'd be left with the feeling that you're lazy or don't have what it takes, or worse, that something is wrong with you.

The reality is, there is nothing wrong with you. In fact, if you have difficulty making changes, then you're actually fine. You're operating exactly how the mind and body are built to operate.

So instead of tackling weight loss head-on, the better option is to prepare and plan for the challenges. That involves learning what habits are, how they operate, ways they manipulate behaviors to keep us stuck in old patterns, and then, develop ways to overcome their manipulative tricks.

This is especially true with concentration. Contrary to the expectations of parents, teachers, and bosses, concentration is not something that can simply be *willed* into being. As with weight loss, *will* can take you only so far before depleting all energy and drive.

Again, the better option is to understand the mechanisms and processes responsible for concentration, including how they work, their strengths and weaknesses, and ways to disengage them. This way, you can be more strategic in your attack.

This is what this book attempts to teach. It offers unprecedented insight into the intricate and complex nature of your mind and body. You will learn so much about the different inner mechanisms and processes that make up you and how to use that knowledge to develop the concentration to do more, have more, be more, and enjoy more in life.

It is by far the best book on developing this critical life skill, especially in this day and age. Honestly, there is no other book like it. You will learn so much about yourself, why you do what you do, and more importantly, why you can't get yourself to do the things you want to do. If this is the level of insight and transformation you seek, keep reading.

Before proceeding, please make sure to download the bonus guide ***Conquer Your Internal Resistance to Make More Money, Have Better Relationships, and Live a Fulfilling Life***. It's free and complements this book's advice to ensure you learn and do more, in less time, and with less effort. You can download your free copy at MindLily.com/ir.

CHAPTER 1 - WHAT IS CONCENTRATION AND WHY IS IT IMPORTANT?

Before diving into the techniques, it helps to understand what concentration is exactly. Concentration is nothing more than the mind's ability to focus its attention on a single thought, idea, or action. It involves directing attention to whatever is relevant in the moment to the exclusion of everything else. This means withdrawing from some things in order to effectively deal with others.

The keywords here are ***withdrawing*** from some things to ***deal*** with others. Right now, you are concentrating. You are narrowing your focus on this book, and simultaneously, excluding everything else that could be done.

Your senses are constantly on, absorbing everything in your environment. Every second, you receive thousands of pieces of information from the senses. To be aware of every sound, sensation, color, and feeling, every moment of every day would undoubtedly make you crazy.

So, no matter how focused you are on the text, your eyes still see the rest of the room. You may be so caught up in what you're doing that you don't hear the phone ringing, but your ears still detect the sound and pass it to the brain.

To an extent, we are always aware of everything going on around us— except that we are not. Somewhere in the brain, a decision is made about what to focus on and what to ignore.

Often, this decision is unconscious. When out to dinner, we hear the people sitting in front of us, but tune out the people at the table behind us. We don't think about doing this, it simply happens.

So, when we pay attention to something, we make a conscious (or unconscious) decision to be aware of that something, while tuning out everything else. We don't get lost in everything around us, but instead direct our senses and thoughts on the task and activity at hand.

This is the essence of concentration.

Benefits of Strong Concentration

Concentration is the single most important skill anyone can develop. Without it, you can't do anything else. You can't read a book, listen to a conversation, understand a lecture, or follow a train of thought. It is a big driver to everything you do and affects every area of your life–every area!

Memory

If you have read my memory improvement book, you know that memory is not possible without concentration. For the brain to store information, it must receive that information. To receive information, focus and attention must be on it. It's impossible to remember a lecture if you're daydreaming through it. At the same time, you can't remember a conversation while mentally grocery shopping. One must concentrate on events and experiences to remember them.

Creativity

The early stages of creativity often require the exact opposite of concentration. They require letting the mind wander and explore seemingly unrelated ideas to tap into unexplored inspiration. However, once inspiration strikes and a creative thought arises, concentration is essential to develop and refine it. Otherwise that great inspiration fades as quickly as it arose.

Productivity

Few things hinder productivity more than the inability to concentrate. Simply put, if you cannot focus, you cannot get things done. There is no way around it. Without focus, a task can feel stressful and frustrating, leading to daydreaming, distraction, and procrastination.

Being Present

Another benefit is that concentration channels awareness to the present. That means you are aware of and able to be in the moment. You are not daydreaming about the future or lost in the past, nor are you thinking about one task while busily performing another. Your presence is on the here and now.

Safety

The most important benefit of concentration is safety. How many times have you been so lost in thought that you drove past an exit, neglected someone call your name, missed an appointment, or lost track of time? These lapses are not life-threatening, of course, but in a dangerous environment, they certainly can be. Even crossing the street in an otherwise quiet neighborhood can be threatening if attention is lost when an erratic driver veers off the road. Concentration is essential to preventing life-threatening mistakes.

As you can see, concentration is a big deal. It's a bigger deal than you can imagine. As discussed, it's particularly vital for memory, creativity, productivity, safety, and even developing healthy relationships. If you are struggling to make positive changes, it is likely because you lack the ability to hold attention long enough to realize those changes.

I Can't Concentrate

Given the previous description, concentration can seem out of reach. It can seem like a skill that isn't available to you and you can't imagine how it ever could. You likely reached this conclusion by overlooking all the areas where you concentrate well, while dwelling only on activities that create difficulty.

The fact of the matter is that everyone has the ability to concentrate. We are always concentrating–all the time. All living creatures, even single-celled organisms, have the ability to sense stimuli. Though it may not seem like it, your concentration is far better than you think.

For instance:

- When you are talking to a friend, you're concentrating.

- When you bury yourself in a favorite hobby, you are concentrating.

- When you can't pull away from cat videos, you are concentrating.

- When you lose yourself in a movie, you are concentrating.

- When you can't stop staring at someone attractive, you are concentrating.

- Even when deep in thought, whatever that thought might be, you are still concentrating.

If you've had any of these experiences, you already have good concentration. You are just not able to direct it. Instead of paying attention to an assignment, you might be daydreaming about the show you watched last night or maybe about becoming a millionaire and never having to do assignments again. Nevertheless, it's still concentration.

The point is, you don't need to learn to concentrate, but instead, take conscious control of this inherent ability. You probably don't decide to get so caught up in a show that you lose track of time or so involved in a conversation that you forget other priorities. These things just happen. You concentrate more on certain activities over others.

By taking conscious control of this inherent ability, you choose which activities to get so caught up in that you lose track of time. You direct focus and attention toward what you need, when you need it most, even if it isn't the most fun or interesting option. To summarize, you can concentrate, you just need to take control of this inborn ability.

Concentration Is a Battle

If you already have the ability to focus, the natural questions that arise are *what makes concentrating on one activity more difficult than on another? Why is it easier to pay attention to cat videos than on homework?*

The answer lies in those mechanisms and processes running in the background. They are designed to prioritize certain activities over others. So, to the mind, certain activities take precedence over others, making them inherently more engaging. Let's explore what these activities are and why they take precedence.

Fun

Anything fun, enjoyable, or pleasurable draws our attention. You may not know this, but pleasure and fun have a purpose. It's to draw ourselves towards what the mind believes is good or healthy. For one reason or another, the mind believes there is some benefit there, so it floods the body with positive emotions that pull us in that direction. Assignments, lectures, and meetings don't give the mind the immediate gratification it seeks, so it doesn't release those arousing feelings.

Threats

Threats and dangers, whether perceived or real, also draw attention. We live in a reality where threats are all around. They include physical threats, social threats, and threats to our resources (such as food, water, clothing, and money). When any of these are at risk, the mind can't help but fixate on the threat until it's resolved. If the mind didn't evolve to fixate on threats, humanity would not have survived.

Inner Drives

Humans have many drives. Some of them include the drive for food, water, sex, security, approval, admiration, wealth, fame, beauty, and much more. Anything that has the potential to fulfill one of these drives will draw our attention.

For example, with a strong drive for financial success, you'll naturally be inclined to pay attention to conversations on investing. It will be effortless. On the other hand, if what you seek is spirituality, dialog about investments will be repulsive. You couldn't pay attention even if you tried. In a different scenario, if the drive is to achieve academic success, then attention will veer towards teachers and reading assignments.

Habits

The previous chapter talked briefly about the role habits play in keeping us in a routine. In their efforts, habits will draw attention toward anything that encourages a habitual behavior, while at the same time, divert attention away from anything that stands in the way of that behavior.

An unhealthy eating habit will always pull attention towards unhealthy meals. You will think about and crave such foods, and even go as far as to schedule the day so eating unhealthy is the only option. At the same time, the habit will make you cringe at the thought of anything that might draw attention away like exercise.

Social Proof

Interestingly enough, many of the things that grab our attention are those that connect us to people or increase our approval or popularity with them. Humans have a ferocious desire to be liked and accepted, and for some, to feel superior to others. For complex reasons, this desire is wired deep into our core.

The mind, therefore, is constantly watching what others are doing. If a group or activity is popular, the mind will make it easier, and even motivate us, to participate in that activity. If others are not involved or if there is stigma associated with involvement, the mind will resist any attempts to engage, even though we may enjoy or derive long-term value from the activity.

This is the reason kids who have a desire to be popular often have trouble concentrating and behaving in school. Their minds seek activities and behaviors that increase their approval rating with peers. If they believe that following the latest fashion makes them *cool*, then their minds will make fashion magazines more appealing than history books. It will be completely unconscious. They won't realize why they are into fashion; they simply won't be able to pull themselves away.

This trend applies to everyone, both young or old. We think we do, want, or like certain things because we enjoy them. The reality is, we take part for the simple reason that the unconscious believes these pursuits will either improve our status with certain individuals, groups, or communities or keep us from being rejected by them. As a result, the enjoyment comes not from the activity itself, but from the feelings of approval, acceptance, belonging, or superiority.

In short, if a goal, hobby, or pursuit makes you *look good* or raises your status, your internal mechanisms will elevate attention in ways you can't imagine. If, on the other hand, involvement reduces standing with peers or colleagues, those very mechanisms will pull attention away as if it were the plague.

Novelty

Have you ever started a project and then lost focus a few days later? Then you began something else, yet lost focus again. You continued this pattern, jumping from one new activity or experience to another.

Why did that happen?

The mind loves the new and different. There's something about having, seeing, doing, hearing, or experiencing something new that makes the hair on our skin stand up. This is why traveling is so much fun. Being in a new city or country, around new people and cultures sparks the senses like fireworks. As soon as the novelty wears off, however, it is as if the flames of desire are blown out.

This also explains why we love buying new things, whether it's a shiny pair of shoes, latest iPhone, or the most recent model SUV. Although we may not need the new shoes, phone, or car, we buy them anyway as having something new is so stimulating. Even if we don't buy them, the mere thought of the purchase stimulates us. Again, as soon as the novelty wears off, so does attention.

And what do we do then?

Naturally, we buy something else!

Novelty's influence on the mind and body is so pervasive, there's a cognitive term for it: *the novelty effect*. It questions whether new treatments or situations improve performance because they work or simply because they're new. Research shows that new treatments often work for no other reason than the fact that they are new. As soon as the novelty wears off, so does the improvement.

These are few of the things our unconscious, internal processes are designed to prioritize. This explains why it's so easy to get lost in a movie than in homework, or more fun to read fashion magazines than history books. It also explains why many prefer cake to exercise, and somehow want what we don't have over what we do.

In effect, concentration is a tug-of-war between what we want to focus on in the moment and what our unconscious is designed to focus on. It involves re-directing attention away from areas the unconscious has placed it to areas where we want or need. In other words, it's about training the unconscious mechanisms to support our conscious desires.

To recap this chapter, concentration is the ability to withdraw from some things to effectively deal with others. It's an innate ability that you share with all organisms, and since it's an ability you already possess, your goal is not to learn how to concentrate, but to take *conscious* control of it. This means directing attention away from where the unconscious is designed to place it and to where you'd like it.

What's Inside

This book is broken into four sections, and each section is divided further into chapters. Each section improves concentration in a specific area and each chapter discusses a specific technique within that area.

Section I addresses concentration training. It presents exercises that give you control of the many unconscious drives and mechanisms running your day-to-day existence. This section is the heart of the book as it rewires your mind to make you innately more attentive. The exercises in this section will both enhance your natural ability to concentrate and put you in more control of it.

Section II covers *in the moment* tools. Developing concentration takes time and effort and even more time to see measurable results. That said, it may take time to realize the benefits from the exercises in Section I. However, for those all-important immediate tasks and goals, you'll need tools that work right away or *in the moment*. The tools offered in this section give you the boost you need in those moments you need it most. They can even propel you to read this book to the end!

Section III tackles distractions, which include anything that sidetrack or divert attention from a given task. Distractions don't necessarily impair concentration, but they can get in the way. In other words, you may already have good focus, but unknowingly allow distractions to keep you from operating at your best. The advice in this section removes unnecessary obstacles in your way to increase the effectiveness of the tips discussed in the previous sections.

Section IV, the final section, addresses lifestyle, routine, and environment. Lifestyle looks at diet, sleep, and physical activity. Routine deals with the best times to do your best work and best ways to manage workload. Environment relates to creating a space and atmosphere conducive to concentration. Everyone is different, so it's important to find a lifestyle, routine, and environment right for you.

Before Getting Started

Before beginning, it's important to address three things.

1. If you're looking for a *quick fix* to end concentration woes, you probably won't find them here. In fact, you won't find them anywhere. Concentration is a skill, and like any skill, developing it requires more than reading a book. It involves applying techniques, doing exercises, and training yourself to resist distractions.

If you are not willing to do these things, then you will not gain the sought-after benefits. Reading and learning seem like they create progress, but they are only one step towards it. If the suggestions are not put to use, they hold no value. The only way to see progress is through action, so apply as many of the suggestions in this book as possible. Jack Canfield, author of the *Chicken Soup for the Soul* series, asserts that *the principles only work if you work the principles.*

2. Second, problems with concentration arise and exist for many reasons. As a result, the road to the solution are many. Some roads are simple and direct, and to a certain degree, common sense. Other paths are substantially more involved, and not so common sense.

Avoid the need to take only the involved and not so common-sense paths. Many fall into the trap of thinking that if they have a complex or debilitating problem, then they need a complex or difficult solution, one that takes time and energy to apply. Since they expect the solution to take effort, they overlook the easy suggestions and focus only on techniques that are difficult, complex, or something they haven't heard or used before.

The reality is if you have a big or complex problem, then more than likely you need a simple and easy solution; one that is easy to apply and that you are encouraged to apply. Applying a technique is what brings results, not procrastinating on it because it's too difficult or time consuming.

Therefore, don't underestimate the simplicity of some of the suggestions in this book and don't focus only on the ones that are new, popular, or demanding. If a suggestion works, use it. If not, move on and try another. Each person is different, so what works for one person may not work for you, and what works for you may only require something simple.

3. Finally, don't expect problems to vanish overnight. You'll see improvement only with consistent practice, and even then, it will be gradual. Instead of seeking immediate gratification from the exercises, work on turning them into habits that supplement your regular routine.

With all the reminders out of the way, let's dive in. The next chapter will discuss the most important piece of the concentration equation, and that is *awareness*. It sets the foundation for all the techniques in this book, so pay attention (no pun intended).

CHAPTER 2 - UNDERSTANDING AWARENESS

To truly enhance concentration, it helps to understand what's going on inside your mind and body. The Introduction talked at length about mechanisms, and the most important mechanism as it relates to concentration is *awareness*.

Awareness is an abstract concept, but more or less, it's where attention takes place. It's where all the thousands of bits of data the mind and body receive filter through to us. In other words, awareness is where information comes to our attention.

Any time you pay attention to something (such as a phone), that something is in awareness. As soon as you stop paying attention to it, it's no longer in awareness. You may still be looking at the phone, but if focus is on a pretty face nearby, that's where awareness resides.

This applies to any activity like reading a book. By looking at the words and processing their meaning, the book is in your awareness. If you are daydreaming while looking at the words, the book is not in awareness. The object of the awareness is instead the daydream.

The body could be seeing, hearing, smelling, tasting, or feeling something, but if it doesn't pierce awareness, attention is not on it. To pay attention to something, it must enter awareness.

The problem is, awareness is limited. There are only so many items that can fit in your awareness at any given moment. You can't simultaneously read a book and admire a pretty face nearby. Think about a bathroom in a large stadium. Only so many attendees can enter at one time.

A bigger problem is many things inside you are competing for awareness. They stem from *verbal thoughts*, *visual images*, and *physical feelings*. At any given moment, you have one of these three circulating through your mind and body, and as such, take up space in awareness. When they take up awareness, it's difficult to concentrate.

Your *verbal thoughts*, *visual images*, and *physical feelings* have a huge impact on concentration. I don't use the word *huge* lightly. Let's take a deeper look at your *verbal thoughts*, *visual images*, and *physical feelings* as they are key to understanding and developing focus.

Verbal Thoughts

Verbal thoughts come from that voice inside your head that is always talking to you. You know that voice that is conversing with you all hours of the day. It is evaluating what you're done, pointing out mistakes you've made, and if you are like most people, criticizing how nothing goes your way, how much of a failure you are, and can't do anything right.

In many ways, this inner voice is like a guide, offering advice about what to do, where to go, how to behave, and what to say. Sometimes it surfaces to remind us of things, like an important meeting. Other times, it goes back and forth to work out a conversation or argument. Still at times, it mulls over decisions or reflects on something happening.

Like the other mechanisms, these thoughts are always there, constantly on. It seems like you are consciously choosing the thoughts you think or are in control of them, but for the most part, they are running on their own. You don't choose or initiate them. Instead, they percolate, like bubbles in a boiling pot.

For some, this is happening very fast with the mind racing through a large number of thoughts and ideas in quick succession. As soon as we become aware of one thought, the mind is already on the third and fourth. You might tell yourself, *Okay, I have to go to the post office*, but before you can figure out what to do there, you remember to stop at the grocery store. Before deciding what to buy at the store, the mind moves on to paying bills, and then on to the next thought, and the one after that.

For others, their mind works such that thinking of one thought triggers a whole host of other thoughts, and those thoughts trigger a host of even more. So, their mind is constantly jumping from one unrelated thought or idea to another. They may be reading about an event that happened in New York, and suddenly, begin thinking about a vacation they took to the city few years back. This may trigger memories of another vacation they took, but to Playa del Carmen, Mexico, where they had a fantastic lobster dinner, and now they're thinking about how great it would be to have lobster. They went from reading to lobster dinner simply from reading the words *New York*.

This kind of jumping happens to all of us, but for some it's more severe. Have you ever chatted with someone who began a sentence on one topic, but ended on something completely different? If so, then you were dealing with a person whose mind is wired such that it randomly skips from one unrelated thought to another.

Still others have minds that fill up like a balloon with so much thoughts that it becomes a cluttered mess. It's not just one set of thoughts racing or jumping, but a whole host of thoughts, ideas, decisions, judgements, and opinions taking center stage.

As you can imagine, any one of these can make it extremely difficult to concentrate. Imagine listening to a lecture with thoughts racing so fast, you can't hold on to anything the speaker is saying. Or imaging receiving instructions from a boss with each instruction triggering a host of random ideas unrelated to work. Furthermore, how difficult would it be to listen to a friend with ten other worries streaming through your awareness?

Worse, you might have all three–*thoughts racing, jumping randomly*, and *filling your head like a balloon*–at the same time. This is the ultimate in challenge and frustration. You want to concentrate, but a dozen other thoughts are competing for awareness, each racing from one to the next, and as each takes center stage, a swarm of unrelated thoughts are triggered, like the climax to a firework show.

Next thing you know, it's impossible to concentrate, and not because your thoughts are racing, jumping, and filling your head like a balloon, but quite frankly, you're exhausted from trying to keep them from racing, jumping, and filling your head.

Visual Images

In addition to thoughts that you *think*, you have thoughts that you *see*. The truth is, we think not just in words, but pictures, and these pictures show up many ways. When you think about something funny, an image of that event will flash in your mind as you laugh about it. Thinking about groceries may blast your awareness with not only pictures of all the items to buy, but the exact brand of each item and its location in the store. If you've never noticed this, you'll likely begin noticing it now.

In addition, the mind regularly replays events from the past. You could be working on an assignment, and suddenly, think about an embarrassing moment from childhood or romanticize about an old flame. If you are not picturing events from the past, then more than likely, you are daydreaming about the future. Maybe you're imagining a beach getaway, pretending to be the popular kid in school, or fantasizing about being the boss at work (or even the boss' boss!).

Sexual thoughts get far less attention in conversations than they do in our minds. As normal, functioning adults, sexual images come in and out of awareness just like any other image. For some, they occur more than any other image.

The bottom line, like verbal thoughts, mental images are constantly running through our heads. Often these images come in and out of awareness so quickly, we hardly notice them. Not only do they indeed come in and out, they are vital for understanding and making sense of our thinking.

For example, if you are trying to figure out what to do today, your mind will quickly scroll through images of possible options. These images will even appear as you select an option. If you decide to call a friend, a mental visual of the friend will appear for a split-second, and even an image of you talking to that friend.

Images are also vital for explaining an idea. In a heated argument with a spouse, images of all the times he or she did you wrong will flicker through your mind as you justify your point. When giving directions to your house, a mental image of your neighborhood will surface as a reference. You might even walk through the mental neighborhood to provide the exact turn-by-turn directions.

Just like verbal thoughts, visual images can run in quick succession, jump randomly from one image to another, or fill your head like a balloon. Some people's awareness is an ongoing mental movie about things that have happened, things they'd like to have happen, fantastical creatures and stories, or as with someone like Albert Einstein, mysteries of the universe.

Physical Feelings

Underneath the verbal and visual thoughts are feelings. Throughout the day, all sorts of feelings are flowing, pouring, coursing, and surging through your body. By feelings, I mean both your emotions and sensations.

To make the distinction clear, emotions include everything from joy, apprehension, surprise, anxiety, excitement, fear, happiness, anger, and yes, attraction. No matter who the person or what the situation, humans are always in some sort of emotional state.

Sensations relate to everything else such as tense muscles, achy back, racing heart, scratchy nose, or even cold hands. When out on a winter's day, you'll *feel* a chilly sensation. A piercing sound creates a different kind of sensation. So, in this context, feelings refer to both **emotions** such as fear and **sensations** such as pain.

If you are not in touch with your *feelings,* you may not realize just how much your thinking is processed through feelings as well. They are instrumental to guiding your decisions and actions. Knowing a meeting is coming up might make you *nervous*, and that *nervousness* may encourage you to prepare more. The weekend approaching might *excite* you, and in that *excitement*, make plans with friends. A *pain* in the body is a sign that something is not right, and that discomfort may encourage a visit to the doctor. In fact, experts in emotional intelligence assert that feelings are the most critical driver to effective decision making.

Like verbal thoughts and mental images, feelings too occur in varying degrees. Some people are very sensitive, so when they feel something, they really feel it. Others cycle through a string of emotions, from one state to another, often without any apparent cause or trigger. One moment, they're excited, the next lethargic, then suddenly anxious. Some experience so many different emotions and sensations in any given moment, they feel they are going to explode.

As you might expect, feelings can also impede concentration. It's difficult to pay attention to any one or thing with feelings incessantly gnawing at you. You might be sitting in class unable to process what the teacher is saying because you are so excited about a date. Or you might be unable to deliver a presentation to a Board of Directors because of intense anxiety. Your lack of focus may be the result of other feelings, such as grief or heartbreak. Feelings of stress such as those from job worries, relationship issues, and health concerns also add to the challenge.

In summary, these are the three main activities in your awareness–*verbal thoughts*, *mental images*, and *physical feelings*. These three elements of *thought* are always there. We are always talking to ourselves, having visions of the past, present and future, and in a mood of one type or another.

What's more is that these thoughts, images, and feelings don't operate alone. They influence and activate each other. If a thought emerges, in all likelihood it is accompanied by an image and/or feeling. Being reminded of an important assignment might trigger anxiety. That anxiety might then elicit mental pictures of the boss yelling at you if the work is not completed on time. So, the *thought* of an assignment sparked *feelings* of anxiety that then spark *images* of the potential consequences.

On the other hand, being asked out might produce feelings of joy. In that blissful state, you may start thinking about how wonderful life is. You might even imagine getting married and raising kids with this person, even though you haven't yet been on a first date! As amusing as this example sounds, we have all let ourselves get lost in such *thoughts* and *images* while under the influence of strong *feelings*.

Sometimes a thought, image, or feeling will arise as a distraction from another thought, image, or feeling. Thinking about homework might trigger feelings of apprehension, dread, or simply not wanting to do it. Instead of dwelling on the unpleasant feelings, the mind will distract you by daydreaming. Now you don't feel so bad. In fact, you feel great. You're a lean, mean fighting machine with Brad Pitt charm and George Clooney charisma.

It's easy to see that thoughts, images, and feelings are intertwined. They don't arise independently, but together. Where there is one, often the other two are lurking behind–either to support the original thought or to distract you from it.

Together, these thoughts, images, and feelings form the basis of all your ideas and decisions. Have you ever had a profound realization or *a-ha* moment that when you tried to explain to someone else, didn't come out quite the way it was worked out in your head? That's because rapid-fire thoughts, coupled with images from past experiences, and a variety of emotions converged to give you that *a-ha* moment. Trying to express those layers with mere words or a single sentence doesn't translate well.

The overarching point of all this is to explain that enormous activity resides within our awareness. The purpose of the activity is to guide our day-to-day lives, from assisting us in our interactions with people to making sense of situations to maneuvering around the environment.

However, when we lose control of our inner thoughts, they become a hindrance not only to concentration, but to overall productivity and success. Random and chaotic thoughts, images, and feelings can cause a frenzy of distractions, and even madness.

It goes without saying, then, that managing these thoughts, images, and emotions is the *yellow brick road* to better concentration. If you could turn off, shutoff, or simply tune out these things at will, concentration and focus would be a breeze.

Think about it, if you didn't have a million thoughts coming up while reading, finishing a book would take little time. If you could press pause on the mental movies while in class, making sense of the teacher would be painless. And if you didn't have a storm of emotions tugging you in every direction, getting things done would be a synch. All aspects of concentration are influenced by these three elements of thought.

It is often said that men tend to be in their heads and women in their emotions. This explanation provides a clearer understanding of what that means. It's the thoughts and images that are in the forefront of a man's awareness, while emotions and sensations at the forefront of a woman's. Both men and women experience all three, though one tends to be more dominant in the awareness than the other.

Now that the foundational elements are addressed, let's begin the concentration journey in the next section.

SECTION II – CONCENTRATION TRAINING

CHAPTER 3 - SELF-TALK

As mentioned in the intro, the chapters in this section discuss concentration training, offering an array of exercises to train your ability to focus. These exercises go deep inside your mind to build concentration from the innermost part of your core.

The fact that these exercises go deep means they take time and patience. Results won't appear the instant you start the exercises. They must be applied frequently and consistently over an extended period to see noticeable results.

Most shy away from anything that takes time and effort as they would rather have the quick fix. As mentioned in Chapter 1, quick fixes for concentration don't exist. Concentration is like taming a wild animal, and that doesn't happen overnight. Although the next section presents some effective *in the moment* tools to quench your need for a quick fix, they will not produce the desired results if the core work in this section is not done.

Think of the training in this section as rehab. Rehabbing a physical injury requires performing exercises to rebuild and strengthen the muscles and tissue around the injury. Without the exercises, the muscles remain weak and perform poorly. In fact, any attempt to use them can cause further injury. Once the muscles are strengthened, however, they perform better and for longer.

The same applies here, concentration muscles need exercise to strengthen and develop. Otherwise, there is only so much they can lift. The suggestions in this section are designed to do just that, so you can focus anytime, anywhere, and in any situation.

This section begins with self-talk, which are statements that you say or think to yourself about the changes you want to have or have happen in life. For instance, if you want to be assertive, you would repeat a statement like, *I am a strong, assertive person.*

You may not think that repeating such a statement can actually make you more assertive, but surprisingly, it can. It's a method used by high performers in many disciplines, whether in school, sports, or business, to enhance their abilities and performance.

Self-talk can be applied this way to improve your ability to concentrate. As an example, you might affirm: *I have strong concentration, I focus on anything I choose.* Repeating such statements, overtime, will build your focus and attention.

How Self-Talk Works

Self-talk improves concentration for two main reasons.

1. First, self-talk is a form of concentration training. With self-talk you are not repeating one statement one time, but rather multiple statements, multiple times. I ask students to list a set of 8 - 12 statements that describe the change they want in an area, and to repeat each statement 10 times, daily.

...every day

...10 times every day

...each statement, 10 times every day.

As you can imagine, this is not easy. After the first few statements, your mind will begin to wander, get lost in other thoughts, not want to do the exercise, or pull you towards other activities. That is, while repeating a set of statements, you might drift to a conversation from last night or an incident that happened at work. Worse, your mind might dislike the exercise so much, it triggers feelings of resistance to make you stop.

In effect, self-talk is an exercise in staying focused on the exercise. It is an exercise in holding concentration on a single thought or activity while keeping the mind from wandering. It is also about resisting the mind's urge to pull your thoughts in other directions. When they are pulled away, it's about bringing them back to the exercise.

So, the mere act of repeating self-talk trains concentration. It builds the strength and endurance to focus on a task for longer and longer periods. Stretching your ability in this area will carry into other areas.

2. The second reason self-talk is so effective is because, overtime, those words will seep into unconscious and rewire your brain to produce better focus. Concentration is not something you do, it's something you are. So, change must be made from the inside and it will naturally manifest on the outside.

I've found the best way to do that is with self-talk. That's because words are powerful. Whether they come from you or someone else, they have a huge influence on the mind. And I mean HUGE!

Words can trigger all sorts of responses in a person. Remember from the last chapter on awareness, I said our thoughts trigger images and emotions. Well, words are thoughts and they trigger emotions that inspire us to act or not.

To illustrate, recently I was having lunch with a friend, who was updating me on what he had been up to since we last spoke. He told me that he was dating someone with things were going really well. He really saw a future with this person.

Then our conversation turned to the power of words. To demonstrate to him the effect words have on us, I told him *You know the girl you're dating, I actually saw her the other day with another guy.* Instantly his expression shifted as he fired *what!* I followed with *Yea, and the way they were talking, it looked they were more than just friends.*

That really set him off! I could see emotions of fear, jealousy, and even anger coursing through his body. I even noticed the thoughts in his head racing. If I were to guess, he was likely thinking *how could she do this to me, I trusted her.*

Here is the thing...I didn't see his girlfriend with another guy. I made that up. They were just words. They had no meaning. In fact, I've never met his girlfriend so I don't know what she looks like to spot her in public.

Yet, and this is a big yet, those words triggered all sorts of responses in him. If I hadn't told him they were made up to demonstrate the effects of words, it would have influenced his action & behavior.

What's more, words can actually create mental barriers. Saying statements like *I'm not smart actually* creates a wall in your mind. The more you say it, the more the wall is reinforced. When you try to do something that requires intelligence, the wall comes up saying *I'm not smart* and stops you dead in your tracks.

If you think about it, majority of your issues in life came from words - parents repeating *you can't sit still*, teachers saying *you can't focus*, peers and bullies making fun of you, bosses saying *your work is no good*. Every one of us at one point in our lives has been told we can't focus, even if we don't remember. Overtime, those words are what created the mental walls of our blocks.

If words created our issues, it reasons that they can change them...and they can. By repeating positive statements, you can change your mental programming to open the gates to do just about anything, including concentrating.

Self-Talk Exercise

Below are 15 statements designed to develop different areas of concentration. Pick 10 or 12 that resonate with the changes you seek, then affirm each statement 10 times, either silently or aloud. Feel free to modify the statements or add in your own to address your unique struggle or need.

Before affirming the statements, it helps to first slow your thoughts and get into a relaxed state. This is important because when you are relaxed, the mind is less resistive to the new messages. This allows the messages to bypass any resistance and enter the depths of the unconscious, where the beliefs reside.

The following is a soothing exercise to calm down and relax. Close the eyes and think about a time when you were calm and at peace—perhaps lying on the beach or hiking in the mountains. Now take a deep breath, hold it for 5 seconds, and exhale slowly while saying to yourself *relax*. Inhale again, hold it for 5 seconds, then exhale slowly while saying *relax*. Do this 3 more times.

Now that you are relaxed, repeat each one of the following statements 10 times.

- I have strong power of concentration.

- I am focused.

- I easily focus on any task or activity I choose.

- My mind is alert and attentive.

- My mind stays on tasks and activities without wandering.

- I pay attention. It is easy for me to pay attention. I enjoy paying attention.

- I calmly focus my full attention on tasks at hand.

- My thoughts are controlled and organized.

- I am free from mental clutter and distractions.

- I naturally ignore distractions.

- I can concentrate on any chore, assignment, errand, goal, or project with ease.

- My mind is aware and observant at all times. It pays attention to what it reads, hears, and sees.

- I hear everything that is said in conversations with others.

- I register every sentence of any material I read.

• I pick up everything that I hear or see.

When repeating the statements, do so with confidence and certainty. That is, affirm the statements as if they were already true, right here and now. Let go of any need or want for the statements to come true, rather accept these words as strongly as you accept the sky is blue.

Also, put positive emotions into the statements. Remember, positive emotions reinforce thoughts that are also positive. This amplifies the statements' power to change beliefs.

More importantly, *focus* on the words. As you learned, it's easy for the mind to wander in all directions. You could be repeating a statement, and without realizing, begin thinking about something else. Keep the mind from straying, always bringing it back to the words when it does.

If your limiting beliefs about concentration are strong, you will experience enormous resistance. With each statement you declare, the mind will counter with *this isn't true, this will never work,* or *concentration will never get better with this stupid exercise.* Ignore the resistance and continue repeating the statements. If you recite the statement, *I enjoy paying attention,* and the mind retorts with *that's not true,* continue repeating *I enjoy paying attention.*

After repeating each statement 10 times, open your eyes and return to the present moment. Do this exercise twice a day for at least 90 days. You will likely see results sooner, but that's the target. Remember, concentration won't improve from doing an exercise only once. It takes repeated practice for the changes to take hold.

This is self-talk in a nutshell. If you have read any of my other material, you know I'm an avid supporter of the technique. Many of my books dedicate an entire chapter to self-talk and I've written an entire book solely on this technique.

That's because I truly believe self-talk is the best, most efficient way to develop a skill. It's a technique I've used personally to overcome a wide range of problems, from memory, anxiety, addiction, productivity, lack of success, and much more. The technique works on many levels to deliver impressive results.

More importantly, the results self-talk delivers are long-term. It rewires the mind to have you naturally acting and behaving in manners you desire. Thus, if you really want to see improvements in concentration, this is the place to start, and it's where you should spend the most time and effort.

Best of all, the technique is simple. It doesn't make heavy physical, mental, or emotional demands nor does it push you to go out and do things. All self-talk requires is to take a few minutes out of the day to repeat a set of statements. That's it. In fact, when it comes to making long-term change, it helps to start with the smallest and simplest step. It doesn't get simpler than self-talk.

So, if there is only one technique in this book that you follow, make it this one. Spend a few minutes each day affirming the above statements. The words have already been provided; all you have to do is repeat them. If you are not willing to do that, then you don't truly desire improvement. You think you do, but deep down you really don't. This is the power of self-talk.

CHAPTER 4 - VISUALIZATION

Visualization is forming an image in the mind. It involves closing your eyes and mentally sketching a person, place, or scene. To demonstrate, close your eyes and picture a long, narrow hallway with a red door at the end. Imagine walking down the hallway, opening the door, and walking out. This is visualization.

As explained in Chapter 2, the mind thinks not only in words, but in pictures. When thoughts or ideas arise, images flicker in the background to make sense of that thought or idea. Most, if not all, verbal thoughts are connected to mental images in some way—even if you are not consciously aware of them.

You also learned that mental images can be a hindrance to concentration. Random images, like a beach vacation, popping in and out of awareness sap focus and disrupt thinking, making it a challenge to follow a train of thought.

Even though mental images can be a hindrance to concentration, you also learned they are vital to the process. To give directions to your house, it helps to call up a mental image of your neighborhood. Concentration requires the ability to intentionally *form* and *hold* mental images that are principal to the task at hand, while keeping irrelevant ones at bay.

There is no better tool to advance this skill than visualization. With this tool, you can practice forming and holding images for longer and longer periods, while simultaneously keeping other thoughts and pictures out of the way. Visualization cultivates a level of mental control that is not possible with any other technique.

Unlike self-talk, which involves simply repeating a set of statements over and over, visualization can be done many ways. The approach depends on the goal and what you seek to achieve. This chapter presents three exercises that use the power of visualization to fine-tune your focus and attention.

Visualization Exercise #1-Holding an Image

The first exercise involves creating a simple shape in your mind and keeping it from moving, changing, or fading.

To start, take a deep breath, close your eyes, and relax. Free your mind of all thoughts—no chanting, mantras, nothing.

Now sketch a shape in your mind, something simple like a circle, square, number, or symbol, so that holding it in place is easy.

Maintain the shape as long as you can without it fading, warping, or changing color.

If the image starts to fade or lose focus, bring it back to focus. If other thoughts creep in, clear them from awareness and bring attention back to the mental image.

What you'll find is that your mind doesn't want to cooperate. It will distort the image, throw other things into the image, or create its own image. The mind may also jump to a completely different thought altogether. All of a sudden, you are thinking about the dry cleaning.

If the mind is really resistant to the exercise, you may even feel physical pain as you battle to maintain focus. Muscles will tense, body will become restless, or you'll feel pressure in and around your head.

Do the best to resist these things. If they occur, center attention and return to the image. Don't get mad, frustrated, or beat yourself up. Just continue as if nothing happened.

This is the KEY to the exercise–to not beat yourself up, but instead to bring yourself back as if nothing happened. Each time you bring yourself back, try to see if you can hold the image a bit longer, then longer, and then a little longer.

The goal is to maintain the shape for a 10- to 15-minute stretch without losing focus or breaking concentration. It takes time, practice, and patience to get to this level, but that's the target.

Once you are able to maintain an image without losing control, you will be able to transfer this skill to other tasks, and hold focus on them with little internal distraction. And if distracted, you'll be able to bring yourself back with ease.

Practice the exercise 10 to 15 minutes each day until you can visualize a shape for an entire 15 minutes stretch. Again, when you can hold that for 15 minutes without other thoughts getting in the way, you will have realized the benefit of the exercise.

Visualization Exercise #2-Manipulating Images

It's great to be able to hold on to a visual thought for longer and longer periods, especially while keeping unrelated ones at bay. However, at times, you want to do more than that; you want to manipulate it as well.

This is especially useful when arranging a space, understanding a process, or solving a complex problem. When decorating a room, for example, being able to mentally arrange and rearrange the room with different furniture can go a long way in finding the ideal setup.

On the other hand, if studying a process, like how atoms form molecules and how those molecules form compounds, the ability to see each particle come together will make it easier to understand how the various pieces fit.

The same goes for solving a problem. Problem-solving involves changing, moving, and manipulating aspects of a puzzle until a solution fits. Manipulating such pieces requires strong mental control.

The following exercise trains you to not only form and hold mental images, but manipulate them as well. Instead of relying on the unconscious to produce the outcomes you desire, this exercise gives you complete control of the process—from beginning to end.

Again, take a deep breath, close your eyes, and become relaxed.

Imagine a line.

Just a simple line.

Hold that image in mind for a few seconds.

Take that line and see it spin clockwise.

Now, reverse the direction, so it is spinning counterclockwise.

Stop the spinning and picture the line splitting in two. You are looking at two lines next to each other.

Visualize the two lines spinning, but in opposite directions.

Stop them again.

Have the two lines split once more so now you are looking at four lines, two horizontal and two vertical.

Have them come together to form a square.

Picture the square rotating horizontally. Watch this play out for about 5 seconds.

Now picture it rotating vertically. Do this for another 5 seconds.

Take this two-dimensional square and watch it turn into a three-dimensional box. Hold the image of this box for a few seconds.

Next, imagine this box as a Rubik's cube, with each of the six sides a different color–orange, yellow, blue, red, green, and white.

Rotate this cube horizontally so you can see all the sides. This is a little bit harder and requires more focus and energy, though do the best to hold it for a few seconds.

After a few seconds, rotate the cube vertically so you can see the top and bottom colors.

Imagine the top of the Rubik's cube rotating right while the bottom rotates left, so now each side is three colors.

Now imagine the left side of the cube rotate up as the right side rotates down, so that now each side is five different colors.

This is getting even more challenging, so stay with this image for a bit.

Let's change up the image so the Rubik's cube is now a gift-wrapped box with a bow on top.

Picture it sitting on a table in an empty room.

Begin furnishing the room. Cover the table with tablecloth, place chairs around the table, place windows on one wall, put paintings on another, and add a door on the third wall.

You might throw blinds on the window, lay carpeting on the floor, and paint the walls a favorite color.

If you can, rotate the room to see it from all angles.

Now see all four walls of the room fall, leaving you standing outside, on top of a bright green hill. The sky is radiant blue with the sun shining brightly.

Look far into the horizon and notice the green fields stretch into the distance.

Now open your eyes and come back to the present reality.

This is a great exercise for developing control of mental images. Like the previous exercise, the mind may not want to cooperate. As you try to form and manipulate the sequence, the mind will attempt to distort or direct it in a different way. If it doesn't do that, it will create its own image.

Worse, each image you create may lead to a completely unrelated thought. For example, picturing the Rubik's cube may take you back to childhood memories of playing with one. Looking in the meadow may remind you of a recent vacation. These memories can trickle into other memories, and suddenly, you've drifted away from the exercise.

Again, do your best to resist any of these responses. If they occur, clear the mind and bring it back to the exercise.

As before, don't get upset or beat yourself up. Just continue as if nothing happened. Remember, this is the key to all the exercises in this book—to *simply bring yourself back as if nothing happened.*

The goal is to get through the entire sequence of images, from beginning to end, without any breaks in focus or without other thoughts, images, and feelings disrupting your efforts.

After accomplishing this, play around with adding additional details. Obviously, you can't add details to the lines, but you can change their color or the colors in the Rubik's cube. You can also adjust the furnishings in the room and notice finer and finer elements of the texture, quality, and patterns of all the items, including the table cloth, blinds, and carpet. However, make sure you can complete the exercise in one sitting before playing around with the details.

More importantly, include only details *you* want in the scenes, not what the mind throws in. If you wish to paint the walls red, but all you see is blue, spend as much time as needed until the color is red. This is important, since the point of the exercise is to mold images around your intentions. You might have to battle with your mind, but remain persistent.

This wraps up manipulating mental images. Like the previous exercise, practice this one for a few minutes a day until you can visualize the entire sequence without interruption.

Visualization Exercise #3-Picturing Yourself

Visualization isn't just for improving concentration; it can improve a whole host of mental and physical skills, talents, and abilities. It is a tool used by a wide variety of people in a wide variety of professions to enhance performance of a wide variety of skills to championship levels.

For instance, visualization is used heavily to improve memory. Memory champions such as Joshua Foer, Ron White, and Dominique O'Brien have used visualization to win both national and international memory competitions. In fact, it's the main weapon in their arsenal.

Sports is another area where visualization is utilized. Athletes use it as a form of mental practice to enhance their performance. In addition to physically practicing an athletic routine, they practice the routine in their mind. They take movements like a baseball swing, basketball shot, or javelin throw and replay the perfect motion of the swing, shot, or throw over and over until it engraves in their mind.

Numerous studies confirm that mental practice enhances performance better than physical practice alone. Not only that, mental practice has shown to enhance performance even *without* physical practice. That is, the mere act of visualizing yourself performing a task improves your performance.

That means visualizing yourself concentrating can develop better concentration. This involves picturing yourself as a person with strong concentration, paying attention in difficult situations and scenarios, and focusing at the top of your ability. Seeing yourself concentrating at the top of your ability leads to you concentrating at the top of your ability.

The following exercise illustrates how to do this precisely.

> Close your eyes once again, take a deep breath, and get back into a relaxed state.

> Think about an area where you have difficulty concentrating. Is it when reading, in meetings, or in conversation? Start with one scenario and picture yourself in that scenario, but this time, fully engaged.

> If you have difficulty paying attention while reading, see yourself reading and paying attention to all the words. See the new you grasping the text of every sentence, paragraph, and section without getting lost in other thoughts. Your mind, thoughts, and awareness

are all aligned on one goal, and that is to be fully immersed in the content and nothing else.

Release any pain or resistance that normally arises when reading. Wash away negative thoughts that suggest reading is dull, boring, or that you are too cool for it. Instead, picture yourself in a state of total pleasure and delight. You enjoy reading as much as any other activity. For you, reading is fun and uplifting, from which much can be gained. In fact, it's effortless.

Now, visualize yourself in the act of reading, with eyes moving across the words, from left to right, one sentence to the next, down the page. As the mental you reaches the end, see him or her immediately flip to the next page with enthusiasm.

Imagine a distraction arises, like a loud noise, a phone call, or an email notification. Still, you remain unfazed. You are not affected by the distraction in the slightest bit, but instead, are completely absorbed by the material. You take attention off the book when you want; it is never pulled away.

Now, let's shift to a different scenario.

Imagine sitting in a class, lecture, or presentation fully engrossed on the presentation. No matter how boring or interesting the content, your eyes are locked on the speaker, taking in everything he or she says. Your mind does not drift or get sidetracked; it is always on the content.

As in the previous scenario, you are calm and free from any physical, emotional, or mental discomfort. Since you are in class, outside worries aren't an issue as you can't do anything in the moment anyway. You let them be. In fact, they don't even come up. If the mind does wander, picture yourself disengage and bring attention back to the speaker like it's no big deal.

Now, visualize a conversation.

Imagine talking to a person one-on-one. That person could be a teacher, boss, co-worker, friend, or even a child. Picture yourself engaged and fully present with this person, listening to everything he or she is saying. You are not just nodding to show you are attentive—you are actually attentive.

Notice how you are not waiting for your turn to talk, but are simply listening. In addition to listening to what the person is saying, you are listening to how they are saying it—whether it is in an angry, annoyed, happy, excited, or sad tone. You withhold any assumptions about what this person might say next, and remain as attentive as you would like others to be with you. In actuality, you are more attentive.

Now open your eyes and come back to the present moment

This exercise works so well because it gives your mind a precise picture of the outcome you seek. A picture is worth a thousand words, so adding a visual image to a self-talk statement like *I have strong concentration* shows the mind exactly what strong concentration looks like.

It's vital to communicate your intentions and desires, and the best way to do that is with pictures. Just because you know what strong concentration looks like doesn't mean that your mind will know as well. Mentally picturing yourself concentrating in different situations and scenarios gives the mind a clear target to model. There is no estimating or guessing. It can proceed directly to cloning the behavior in the image.

This sums up the third way to use visualization to advance concentration, imagining yourself operating at the top of your ability. This exercise presented few of the more common scenarios, though feel free to insert situations and challenges unique to you.

You can imagine working on a dreadfully boring project for school, a mind-numbingly repetitive task at work, or any other situation where you normally have difficulty. That can also include listening to a coach, watching a movie, studying for an exam, and even taking an exam. As you imagine the situation, observe yourself actively engaged and involved while effortlessly ignoring potential distractions.

These are the three ways to apply visualization. The first had you sketch a mental picture of a simple shape or object while keeping it from moving, changing, or fading. The second took that one step further to manipulate those images. The last taught you to use visualization in ways athletes and top performers do.

One final note, when it comes to visualization, you may not *see* an actual image or see one as clearly as it looks with open eyes. Often, you'll just get a feeling or sense of what you are trying to visualize and imagine. That's okay. It still requires focus, so you still reap the benefits.

CHAPTER 5 - WORKING WITH THOUGHTS, IMAGES, AND FEELINGS

Hopefully you're starting to see there is a lot going on inside your mind and body. You are not this whole conscious, walking, talking, being you once assumed, but rather a complex set of systems and processes, and one of those processes is awareness. Inside your awareness flows verbal thoughts, mental images, and an assortment of emotions and sensations.

You also learned that this activity, although critical to day-to-day function, can severely hinder concentration. Like an overstuffed drawer, only so much can fit within our awareness at one time. Thus, successful concentration requires clearing out space in the drawer to make room for the priority at hand.

The problem is, you cannot simply get rid of these thoughts, images, and feelings nor stop them from running. They are always there, and if not in the foreground, then in the background. They are part of who you are, what makes you human, and in many ways, defines your personality. Therefore, they can't ever be totally eradicated.

Although you can't completely eradicate the activity in your awareness, you can learn to work with them, which is the key to managing this mayhem. This chapter teaches exactly that. It presents three exercises to develop better control over what enters awareness and to ensure what enters is what you want.

Exercise 1 - Ignoring Thoughts, Images, and Feelings

This first exercise trains you to tune out and ignore the inner chaos. As mentioned, our inner thoughts can at times become overly active, reeling every which way. This is especially true in tense, stressful situations.

When they get this way, little can be done to silence or control them. The mind is in a frenzy and you are not able to step back and calm it down. Even when trying, your efforts don't prove useful. In these situations, it's best to simply ignore the experience the mind is creating.

That's the goal of this exercise—to maintain focus despite all the mental commotion. It is like putting on blinders; mental distractions and diversions are there, but they are tuned out.

> To begin, pull out a sheet of white paper and draw a black dot about the size of a peanut in the center. Tape the paper on the wall in front of you.
>
> Whether you are standing, sitting in a chair, or on the floor for this exercise, make sure the dot is at eye level. You don't want to strain your vision by having to look up or down at it.
>
> Close your eyes and take a few deep breaths until you feel relaxed.
>
> Open the eyes and look at the black dot. Keep the gaze there without looking away. If attention (or eyes) wander, bring it back.
>
> Maintain attention on this dot for as long as you can. As you do, ignore any thoughts, images, or feelings that arise. The goal is not to shut them out, but to simply ignore them.
>
> Since there is nothing particularly interesting about staring at a dot, the mind will want to wander. The exercise is a test of will to heed a subject despite the mind's desire to wander.
>
> When the mind does wander, it will wander all over the place. At first, you might start reminiscing about the past, planning for the

future, reflecting on a conversation, preparing for an argument, or analyzing everything going on in your life and the world.

You may think something like *this is a stupid exercise, I don't want to do it*, followed by an urge or desire to do something else.

If you have a habit of being self-critical, you will drift into self-criticism. You'll start thinking about all the mistakes you've made in life followed with thoughts like, *I'm so stupid. Why did I do this? I can't do anything right.* If your criticizer is really bad, it will downright berate you, even blasting your efforts on this exercise.

At some point, you may start thinking about how busy you are and how you really don't have time for this drill, followed by a dialogue about the need to get back to work—that you'll finish the exercise when time frees up. Or your awareness might shift to a funny incident like your dog falling off the couch or a friend stubbing his toe.

In addition to these visuals, you might start imagining yourself somewhere else or doing something else, like at the gym working out, at the park playing ball, or the mall shopping for shoes. You might even have flashbacks of a similar exercise, maybe one you did as a child, when your parents put you in time out.

At times, you will get so lost in your head that you will forget you are doing this exercise. Suddenly you will wake up, as if from a dream, only to realize you are supposed to be paying attention to the dot in front.

On the other hand, you might be so caught up in the exercise, you begin thinking about how to do it better, and even question whether you are doing a good job. You may get lost in *trying* to concentrate on the dot, instead of actually concentrating on it.

If you manage to hone in on the dot, your thoughts may start talking directly to you. They may ask, *hey, why aren't you paying attention to me?* That may go from asking why you are not paying attention, to requesting to pay attention, to demanding that you pay attention, to ultimately getting upset that you are not paying attention.

In addition to upset, other feelings may arise. You might start to feel uneasy or restless. You may feel a pull towards something else, like an urge to check email, call a friend, or go to the bathroom. Or you may get bored, tired, and sleepy. Worse, you could feel physical pain.

These are some directions the mind will wander, though this is just a sample. There are a thousand-and-one ways thoughts, images, and feelings rob focus. Understanding exactly how they do will put you in better position to not be seduced by them.

So, keep a watchful eye on your thoughts attempting to stray in any of these directions. Don't let them get in the way of concentration. As soon as you catch yourself thinking about something else, direct focus back to the dot and keep everything subordinate to it. The one and only goal for the exercise is to fix attention on the black dot as you tune out everything else.

In addition to the previously mentioned diversions, it is possible to see the dot's shape or color change. It may even disappear and then reappear. All of these are typical responses to staring at something for an extended period. Again, don't allow these tricks to break concentration. They are only tricks designed to lead you astray.

As with the previous exercise, spend 5 to 15 minutes per session. Of course, this will be challenging in the beginning. Your thoughts will likely stray numerous times a minute, if not more. Regardless, continue to bring attention back.

Over time, the ability to isolate awareness on this spot will expand, and hence, your ability to isolate awareness on any other task or activity. More importantly, the exercise will clue you into how your thoughts stray so you can catch them before they actually lead you astray.

Exercise 2 - Clearing Thoughts, Images, and Feelings

The last exercise trained concentration by holding focus on a single point while attempting to ignore other thoughts, images, and feelings. In this exercise, instead of ignoring the inner thoughts, you will attempt to stop them from arising.

Being able to ignore thoughts proves useful in certain situations and for a certain amount of time. However, it doesn't eliminate the underlying problem. It simply trains you to tune out all the diversions and distractions running through your mind.

A much more useful skill is to not have these diversions in the first place. Having less diversions entering awareness means less getting in the way of concentration, which means significantly easier time concentrating. Often, it will feel effortless because there isn't this battle with your inner thoughts for space in awareness. You can naturally engage in whatever activity is ahead.

To start, close your eyes again and take a few deep breaths.

Then open them and bring attention back to the dot.

As you stare at the dot, clear the mind of all thoughts, images, and feelings. Empty awareness so there is nothing there but a blank space—a void, vacuum, or emptiness. Don't think about anything or let anything enter.

The moment a thought enters awareness, disengage it immediately. Interrupt whatever conversation, picture, or sensation that tries to seep through the cracks. Do not ignore, observe, or get lost in what comes up. Simply, clear it from mind.

It might at first be difficult to know how to do this, but it's like when you push away an embarrassing or unpleasant memory. However, instead of trying to contain, restrain, or suppress the thought in any way, the aim is simply to stop it from continuing. When you notice a thought, put a break on it and clear it from awareness.

Think of a teacher wiping a chalkboard. As soon as the mind begins writing on the board, stop the writing and wipe away what was written. When something else shows up, wipe it away again. Keep doing this so the board always remains clear.

It helps to know exactly how the mind will battle with your efforts to continue writing on the board. First, as soon as you stop one thought from arising, another one will immediately take its place. As soon as that one is disengaged, yet another is waiting in line.

Also, these thoughts and feelings don't make a grand entrance, nor do they announce that they are showing up. They appear without warning. Often, they creep in slowly before becoming full blown.

You might be staring at the dot thinking about how it resembles a coffee bean. Coffee bean leads to thinking about groceries. That in turn triggers a reminder to stop at the store. Suddenly, you're mentally grocery shopping. The mind went from a seemingly harmless association to a fully engaged thought.

Not only do thoughts creep in slowly, they are sly in their approach. As you work on removing one thought, another begins to sneak in. By the time you remove the first thought, the second is becoming full blown.

If attempts to head off the second thought is successful, you might find a third underneath. The third was developing while you were working on removing the first two. Since the third thought had more time to develop, all of a sudden you are fully absorbed without knowing how it happened.

Worse, the first or second thought you disengage will want to come right back. As soon as they are disengaged, they will jump back in line for the next opportunity to sprout.

At times, you will have two or more thoughts come up simultaneously. If you are not careful, you may put effort on erasing one while the other matures. In fact, you could be trying to remove one thought while fully engaged in another. That is, you might be thinking, *wow, I'm doing such a good job with this exercise!* but unbeknownst to you, that statement itself is a thought. By continuing down that road, the mind is not clear. It is still engaged.

This leads to the next point.

Some thoughts, on the surface, don't seem like thoughts, but they are. Any observations about the exercise like what to do, what not to do, how to do it, or whether you are doing a good job seem perfectly okay to think about and have in awareness. Although they may be helpful in doing the exercise, they go against the exercise. In effect, awareness remains occupied.

At times, you may think you have cleared your mind, so in that moment, you'll get excited about how there are no thoughts in awareness, question how long it will last, or wonder about the next thought that will arise. Again, that's still thinking. This will happen quite often where you are convinced the flow of thinking has stopped, yet are still thinking.

Beware of these patterns, stages, and ways thoughts enter awareness. Notice whether they creep up slowly, sneak through the back door, emerge simultaneously, or show up disguised. Whatever their mode of entry, don't allow them to gain traction. Nip them at the bud so they don't have the opportunity to blossom.

If you are like most, this exercise may prove more challenging than the last. It's one thing to ignore what enters awareness, but a whole another to kick them out. Attempting to do so creates feelings of discomfort, resistance, and even pain because our internal processes don't like to be disengaged.

They have become so *habituated* to operating a certain way that they want to continue the process. In fact, they need to continue the process so much so that they will mount an offensive to counter your efforts.

That's why you will feel discomfort and pain. The pain is the internal processes resisting your efforts. So, this exercise requires sitting through more physical and mental discomfort, especially in the beginning.

A great way to relieve the pain is by disrupting it as you would any other thought. As a pain arises, locate where in the body you feel the pain or resistance and break the signal. Don't give it a chance to persist or get stronger.

Also, disengage more than just the verbal thoughts. Most people direct efforts strictly on their verbal thoughts with this exercise, because for most of us, that is our dominant form of thinking. Remember that thinking consists of mental images and physical feelings as well. Make sure to interrupt, disengage, and clear the mind of all forms of thinking–chatter, images, movies, tension, tightness, cringing, and any other emotions or sensations.

And if you recall from Chapter 2, a verbal thought in awareness likely means related images or feelings are lurking around. By eradicating the verbal thought, you'll notice a corresponding image or feeling appear. When they do, be ready to interrupt and clear them from mind. Don't get caught off guard or become too confident that it is completely gone, otherwise you will be taken away like a carpet ride.

To reiterate, you can never eliminate all your thoughts from awareness or have it be completely blank, at least not for an extended period. That's not possible for even the most devout monk. Luckily, that is not the purpose of the exercise. The purpose is to simply clear the mind of thoughts as they arise.

It's like driving in a heavy storm. The rain is falling on the windshield, but the wipers clear it away. There is never a moment when the rain stops; however, because the wipers constantly wipe away the falling water, the view remains *clear*.

It's the same with this exercise. Like a heavy storm, thoughts will pour relentlessly into your awareness, blurring your view of what's important. By constantly removing these thoughts, awareness stays clear, despite the endless downpour. You are not pulled in by any specific drop or thought.

In fact, as you notice each one and gently clear it away, you fall into a rhythm of thoughts arising and being removed. The rain is still coming down, the drops are still falling, but attention is no longer on that. It is drawn rather to the rhythm and the blank awareness generated by it.

This is clearing in a nutshell. With it, you try to keep awareness void of thoughts, images, and feelings. There are no mantras to repeat, no shapes to visualize, or anything else. When any of that arises, disrupt or disengage from it and go back to the black dot on the wall.

Practicing this exercise regularly develops an automatic response to clear the mind whenever the need to concentrate arises. It becomes a natural process. Worries on your mind? No problem! Disengage and bring it back to the objective at hand. If worries resurface, disengage and return to the activity again. The more you do, the easier it will be to disengage.

More importantly, this exercise eliminates many of the erratic, unpredictable, and often violent thoughts, images, and feelings running through your awareness. It does it by breaking their habituated pattern. As you know, the content and flow of what resides in awareness is a giant habitual mess. Repeatedly clearing away the items chips away at the habit's crushing grip. The more the habit is disrupted, the more its grip is weakened.

Over time, many of these elements of thoughts simply stop surfacing. As a result, there is no longer a struggle or need to manage these things because they don't arise. Awareness becomes less congested and more open to receive, allowing you to think clearly and easily absorb information that comes your way.

To be honest, much of our inner thoughts have little use anyway. Majority of it is nonsense, filling the head with pointless daydreaming, fantasizing, criticizing, and arguing. Somethings that come through are useful, but most are not.

What's more, much of it is incredibly repetitive–that is, we wallow in the same thoughts, over and over. Over time, the mind, and hence you, become accustomed to thinking, seeing, and feeling a certain way, as if your mind is set on repeat. You may not realize, but the repetition of these thoughts is what is causing the same events to play out in your life.

The more you clear awareness of these unimportant thoughts, the more you can pay attention to the ones that matter, in the moments that matter. If done correctly, this exercise can drastically reduce the amount of inner distractions and diversions, while toning down their speed and intensity. In moments when distractions do get through, you'll have the self-control to disengage them before they become a disruption.

An added benefit of this exercise is that it can help you overcome long-standing mental and emotional blocks like stress, nervousness, and even low self-esteem. Much of our anxiety and self-esteem come from our pattern of thinking and feeling. Since this exercise breaks these patterns, they stop creating such a mental and emotional state.

What you will realize is that feelings of stress, nervousness, anxiety, and the shyness, insecurity, and low self-esteem that underlie them are merely emotions. They are not you, but because you've become so habituated to feeling them, you've come to accept them as you. With this exercise, you can disrupt the cycle, and over time, break free from its chains. This reduces tension and anxiety to be calmer, more centered, and present and that's what concentration is all about.

The technique works as a great *in the moment* tool as well. Anytime there is a feeling of dread, apprehension, or just plain not wanting to do something, simply clear that feeling. Wash away the thoughts and associated attitude and notice how it instantly engages you in the task.

Like the previous exercises, spend 5-15 minutes each day. You will not be able to hold empty awareness for the entire time, so like wipers in a car, focus only on clearing your mind. Anything that lands is wiped away.

Exercise 3 - Observing Thoughts, Images, and Feelings

With this exercise, instead of ignoring or removing your thoughts, you are going to pay attention to and observe them. That's right, this time you are going to pay attention to them.

A good analogy for this is cloud watching. Ever lay around on a warm summer's day, watching clouds pass across the sky? You don't fret about where the clouds are going, trying to get rid of them, nor making them into what you think they should be. More importantly, you don't engage or react to them in any way.

It's the same with this exercise, don't try to control, ignore, or get rid of your thoughts, simply observe as they pass through awareness. A thought comes and goes, then another comes and goes. Simply notice them pass. Allow a thought to surface, run its course, then go away.

The goal is to become increasingly *aware* of what's in your awareness. This is crucial because your thoughts and feelings want to be noticed. As you learned, they are there to assist and support you. To do that, they have to communicate with you. In turn, they want that communication to be heard.

The problem is most of us are not in touch with our inner thoughts and feelings. Often, we tune or shut out what enters awareness. Growing up, no one emphasized this important skill as society would much rather have us pay attention to them than ourselves. Then, as soon as they have our attention, they try to sell us something.

Restraining or suppressing thoughts and feelings doesn't make them go away. It only makes them stronger. As mentioned, our thoughts want our attention. When we don't pay attention, they try harder by getting stronger and louder. As their effort builds, so does our effort to shut them out.

Overtime, this back-and-forth in and of itself can become a habit. A thought or feeling arises and our automatic response is to tune it out. The feeling counters by getting stronger and more disruptive. This makes us want to shut it out even more. Next thing you know, the mind is bubbling, bouncing, and jumping because this unconscious, back-and-forth pattern is stirring underneath.

To break this cycle, it's important to pay attention to the items in your awareness from time to time. Doing so ease the mental load because all your thoughts and feelings ever wanted was to be noticed and acknowledged. Once they are, they become less restless, chaotic, and jumpy and more calm and still. When the mind is still, so is concentration.

I have a friend whose son used to be very hyper and needy. He sought attention from his mom 24 hours a day. One day, she realized her son's restless behavior was simply a need for attention. Not a mere acknowledgement that *hey I'm here*, but rather being fully present and engaged with him. What she noticed is that by spending an hour or so being fully with him, his restlessness went away.

Interestingly, the son could tell when his mom wasn't fully there. If she interacted with him with other thoughts on her mind, while texting or watching TV, he knew she wasn't fully there. So, she put all that to the side and focused strictly on him for a full hour. The rest of the day, he was calm, could be on his own, and didn't bother her much.

This is similar to our inner thoughts and feelings. In fact, one can argue the boy's need for attention stemmed from his own thoughts and feelings. The mom ignoring his feelings only made them grow stronger and louder, making him more restless and needy.

Paying attention to our thoughts and feelings naturally quiets them. In fact, you can undo long-standing worry, anxiety, regret, and guilt simply by paying heed to the worry, anxiety, regret, and guilt. That's all they were wanted. Doing so can significantly reduce their intensity. Often, they go away like magic, never to surface again. And if they do resurface, not as intensely.

So, let's go inward once again.

> Close your eyes one last time, but this time keep them closed (no need to look at the dot).

With closed eyes, become *aware* of your *awareness*. Notice what's percolating inside. What are you thinking, what are you seeing, what are you feeling? Whatever it is, don't act or react. Simply notice, acknowledge, and observe.

If you are evaluating a decision, let your mind evaluate. If you are daydreaming, allow yourself to get lost. If angry, great. If worry arises, this is the time. Whatever it is, just observe.

While observing, consider why these things are coming up. If you are evaluating a decision, what are you aiming to achieve? If lost in a dream, what is it that you crave? If angry, what is not right? If worry is the trouble, what are you hoping to avoid? Look for deeper meaning and clues to the thoughts and feelings that emerge.

If you are like many, you may have a negative inner voice that criticizes, scolds, and downright puts you down. Now is the time to let that voice out. Allow it to express all its anger, frustration, and disgust with you. For the moment, don't accept, reason, or defend yourself. Let it express what it needs.

On the other hand, if the frustration is with the world, allow that frustration to vent. Don't rationalize away the feeling by thinking that you are overreacting or there is no reason to get worked up. You are already worked up, so acknowledge the emotion without attempting to restrain or control it.

What you will notice is each of our feelings has a voice, and that voice verbally expresses that feeling. You must pay attention to the feelings in order to hear the voice. Whether the feeling is anger, worry, or loathing, pay close attention so you can hear and process what it is saying.

If the feeling is anger, the voice will sound like *I hate this! Oh, I'm so mad. I can't believe that.* This will be followed by negative things you want to do or have happen to the person that triggered the anger.

The voice of worry will sound like, *I don't know what to do. What if I screw up? This will never work!* Followed with possible consequences if things don't go as planned.

The voice of self-loathing will sound more like *I don't like myself. I hate that I did that. Why can't I do anything right?* Then you'll be reminded of all your past mistakes and screw-ups, so you know full well why you're such an idiot and can't do anything right.

Such voices exist with all your other feelings as well, from rejection and sadness to acceptance and joy. Again, it helps to notice and acknowledge them to hear what they are saying. Understanding what they are saying or communicating goes a long way to taming them.

Since feelings have voices, much of your mental and visual chatter are a result from some underlying feeling. If engrossed in thoughts of *I hate this, I hate that*, that means you are angry. On the other hand, dialogue like, *this won't work, I can't do that* is a sign of worry or fear. You may not be aware of the fear, but it's lurking underneath the voice or image. Keep an eye out so when the feeling shows itself, you don't unknowingly shut it out.

As you do this exercise, stay with a thought or feeling for as long as it remains in the forefront. Don't try to change or rush through them. Whatever arises, let it arise for as long as needed. Refrain from pushing anything away, even if it is a thought or feeling you don't like.

On the other hand, if your mind is bouncing randomly from one thought to another, allow that as well. For this exercise, there is no need to stay with anything particular. It's okay to let the mind go where it goes, without pushing or pulling it in any direction. The only goal is to observe the pushing and pulling.

If the mind is bouncing, it may mean that many of the things in your awareness are a distraction to feelings you are trying to avoid. Many feelings like shame, embarrassment, ridicule, stress, nervousness, anxiety, loss, and grief downright suck. Sometimes they suck so much that not even your unconscious wants to experience them. Consequently, the unconscious will do what it can to divert your attention from them.

It will do this by throwing so many other thoughts, images, and feelings into your awareness, that you can't see what's underneath. You will be in such a frenzy with all the errands to run, people to meet, conversations to have, and shows to watch. Any time there is a lull in the day, you'll have an insatiable urge to do something else. If you don't, your head will fill up with useless chatter.

An uncontrollably busy mind, to the extent that it is not pleasant, usually means that unacknowledged feelings are present that you or your mind is trying to avoid. As stated, unacknowledged feelings don't go away, they just get stronger and more disruptive. Eventually, they can become so disruptive that they destroy all ability to concentrate.

In this light, as unpleasant as some feelings are, it's important to not run from them. More on this will be discussed in Chapter 23, though understand that no matter how painful some feelings are, allowing them to surface is the golden road to improved concentration.

These are some ways to manage your inner thoughts, images, and feelings and keep them from getting in your way. One is to ignore the activity in your awareness, another is to clear anything that arises as they arise, and the last is to notice and observe everything that arises. All three present unique benefits and are worth the time and effort as they deal directly with the elements of awareness most influential to concentration.

CHAPTER 6 - RETRIEVAL

A challenge many experience with concentration is that they are trapped inside their head. They get so lost in their thoughts or habituated pattern of thinking that they miss what's happening around them. Others experience the opposite. They are so distracted by the world around them, they can't follow their own train of thought.

Healthy concentration requires the ability to both pay attention to what's going on inside your head, as well as what's going on outside – not necessarily at the same time, but in the right moments. The exercises in the next two chapters will help you do that. This chapter will introduce you to retrieval, a technique that also boosts memory, to help you better follow what goes on in your head.

Retrieval is the act of calling to mind information from memory. It basically involves recalling information you have read, heard, or watched without re-reading, re-hearing, and re-watching the material again. For example, after reading a chapter in a book, retrieval entails closing the book and thinking about everything you read. Or after a class ends, you call to mind everything the teacher discussed.

The challenge with retrieval is that it can be extremely difficult and sometimes painful to do. The activity requires a good deal of inward focus and attention to review and extract what the mind took in. Naturally, the mind would much rather get lost in its habituated pattern of thinking than do this exercise.

That's why many hate studying and taking exams, and that's also why answering questions that come easy is more enjoyable than having to strain for the answers. Straining to think of answers requires using the mind in ways we are not accustomed. It can be downright irritating to wrestle with mental habits to search our memory bank.

That's what makes retrieval such a perfect exercise. It forces you to train focus and attention on a difficult mental task. It also extends your ability to stay with thoughts and ideas to better probe, explore, and examine them.

Another benefit of retrieval is that it encourages the mind to naturally be more attentive throughout the day. If the mind knows it will be called on to retrieve the events of the day, it will put more effort into paying attention to those events during the day. This is the real advantage of retrieval. It develops the internal motivation—one that stems from the unconscious—to pay attention. This automatically improves focus of everything you do.

The side-effect of retrieval is a boost to memory, which is important because concentration and memory go hand in hand. If you are seeking to improve concentration, you are doing so not just to engage more in the moment, but to better remember those moments. Retrieval does both.

The technique can be applied many ways, and one way is to start with a daily review of everything that happens in your day. Each evening, spend 5 to 10 minutes thinking about everything that happened in the day. Start from when you wake up in the morning and work your way into the evening, retrieving as much detail in between. Here is a walk through:

> First think about what you did when waking up. Did you get up right away or linger in bed? If you lingered, what were you thinking while lingering?

> What happened after you finally managed to get out of bed? Did you throw on clothes and leave home or did you shower and get ready first? If getting ready was step one, what did that involve? Go beyond the daily routine and center your efforts on the specifics of that day.

> Did something happen that normally doesn't? Maybe the toilet paper ran out, or maybe you spilled mouthwash. Did toothpaste dribble on your new shirt? Call up the unique moments since those tend to get lost easily.

> What did you do next? Like most people, you ate breakfast. Did you make breakfast or go out? If you ate out, recall where you went

and the details of that place. Think about where the restaurant was located, how the employees treated you, and where customers sat.

If you made breakfast, recall what that involved, from grabbing food from the pantry and fridge to pulling out pots and pans to finally serving the meal. Was the meal consumed alone or with others? If with others, with whom and what was the topic of discussion? Recall what each person said and in the exact order.

What was on the agenda after breakfast? You either went to school, work, or ran errands. Before retrieving the specifics of where you went, retrieve the specifics of how you got there–by foot, bike, bus, car, or some combination. Recall as much of the journey including the route you took, the road blocks or detours that were encountered, and unusual incidents that occurred like tripping on the sidewalk or getting caught in the rain. If the journey involved others, recall the interaction with them.

Continue the exercise for the rest of your day, reviewing as thoroughly as possible what you did, where you went, and everything that happened. Don't just note that you went to lunch, but specify where you went and with whom, what you ordered, where you sat, and what happened along the way. At the office, think about all the tasks completed, errands ran, projects led, and meetings attended.

Make sure to retrieve the events in order. Don't jump to any memory that surfaces. If memories of dinner erupt while reviewing the events of lunch, set dinner to the side. Recall details of dinner only after you've finished recalling everything before.

The same applies to individual events or encounters. That is, while reflecting on lunch, don't jump back and forth between what happened during that hour. Start with what happened first (you ordered food), move to what happened next (found a place to sit), and only then to the events that transpired after (conversation with colleagues).

Staying in sequence can be a challenge because some aspects of the day may not surface as easily or as clearly as others. In those moments, the mind will want to jump to a point that is easier to remember.

Resist such temptations by sticking with the moment and trying harder to bring it to mind. Going out of sequence will only encourage focus to jump and isolate memories that are easy to remember, preventing you from putting the extra effort necessary to remember the details in between.

If you find retrieval difficult to do, that means you have become habituated to thinking a certain way. Your automatic processes are doing the thinking and are battling with your attempts to do something else. You will have to exert extra effort and really impose your will to go against the habituated process in the beginning.

On the other hand, if you are not able to recall anything, that means you are not focused on much of what you do day-to-day. You are coasting through life on autopilot, and as a result, absorbing very little. If that is the case, then this and the exercise in the next chapter are even more important for you, as they will train you to be more aware of what you are doing and is happening around you.

A helpful tip is to close your eyes during the exercise and visualize everything that happened. If other images get in the way, use the suggestions in the visualization chapter to focus only on the images you want while keeping those at bay.

The great thing about retrieval is that it doesn't require much. There's no need to be at a desk, in front of a computer, or on the phone. Unlike the previous exercises, this one doesn't involve going deep or inward either. All it requires is to think about and call to mind as much detail from your day. That means, retrieval can be done anytime and anywhere–while waiting in line, during a commute, and in between meetings.

Even more, you don't have to wait until the end of the day to reap the benefits of retrieval. You can apply it throughout the day to improve focus and attention on specific tasks and activities that create challenge.

If, for example, you have difficulty paying attention while reading, consider stopping every few pages or chapters to recall what you just read. Summarize as much of the text as possible before reading further. Again, if the mind knows it will be immediately called on to recite a passage, it will be more motivated to pay attention while reading that passage. This will keep you intentionally engaged in the material.

You can also apply retrieval in interactions. Right after a conversation or meeting, mentally review the important points that were addressed or the important tasks added to the agenda. Or after a phone conversation, replay everything that was discussed in the call.

Again, if you are unable to remember such details is an immediate sign that you were not paying attention. This will encourage you to revisit any notes and be more attentive next time. And more attentiveness next time is really the end goal.

This sums up retrieval, a simple exercise that has a colossal impact on both concentration and memory. Regularly retrieving the day's events and experiences encourages the mind to be more attentive to them, but more importantly, gives you the ability to follow your train of thought from one to the next without distractions from the world outside.

CHAPTER 7 - ATTENTION TO DETAIL

The last chapter introduced the idea that some people are trapped inside their head. They get lost in their thoughts and habituated pattern of thinking, so the world passes them like wind in the trees. Therefore, they miss important information coming at them.

A powerful solution to this problem is to pay attention to details. This means opening your awareness to your surroundings and observing finer and finer features and aspects of things that you never cared to observe or notice before. This can apply to anything, anytime, and anywhere.

While walking in a neighborhood, for example, paying attention to details involves noticing features of the homes like their shape, size, and color. It also involves noticing the lawn, the fence around it, and even the styles of the homes, whether they are one-story or two, split-level or ranch, as well as traits that you haven't noticed in other homes.

By learning to pay attention to details, guess what you are doing? You are learning to pay attention. You are training yourself to get out of your head and notice the world around you. Like any exercise, the more you do it, the more you can engage with the world outside yourself. Over time, you'll find that without even trying, you are more attentive to what is going on, with little effort or strain on your part.

That means during a lecture, instead of getting lost in your head, attention is on the speaker. While reading a report, you're instinctively focused on the words. When in conversation, the mind is automatically hearing and making sense of what the other person is saying.

Let's walk through examples of how this can be done.

If you are out for a stroll, open your awareness to the surroundings. A good place to start is with the sidewalk. Look down and notice how wide it is and how far the dividing lines are spaced. Does the sidewalk look clean or dirty, old or new? Pay attention to the cracks down there, maybe even count the number of cracks as you walk. Or, simply follow the cracks from where they begin to where they end.

While walking, pay attention to the places you pass. If walking past stores and shops, read their signs and advertisements and notice the products or services they offer.

Do the same with other buildings, whether an apartment, office, or warehouse. Look at the color, height, and the type of material with which they are made–brick, stone, wood, concrete, plastic, or metal. Are there windows? If so, how big are they? Can you determine the number of floors by counting the rows of windows?

Go beyond your eyes by tuning in to your other senses. Listen to the sounds–birds chirping, branches swaying in the wind, the crackling of dried leaves, the buzzing of car engines, and people talking.

Often outside noise tends to blend together to form a loud humming. We become so accustomed to it, we forget it's there. Bring this humming into the forefront and strip each layer to dissect all the individual sounds that make up this humming. If indoors, pay attention to the hum of electricity, air conditioner, and the refrigerator, as well as other sounds like water pipes and noisy neighbors.

As it relates to smells, pick out unique scents and odors in the air. Notice how these scents differ from one location to another. You might notice a particular scent at home, but something completely different in a car, office, restaurant, and even different places outside like the beach or park.

Of course, take note of the people that pass. Observe whether they are male or female, young or old, student or professional. Examine their clothes from their shirt, jacket, and hat to pants, shoes, and belt. How are they carrying themselves, are their heads down or are they looking up?

Anytime you catch yourself in your head or habituated pattern of thinking, clear those thoughts and bring attention back to your surroundings.

As mentioned, you can pay attention to details anytime and anywhere, even in the bathroom. When brushing your teeth, observe the taste and texture of the toothpaste, bristles of the toothbrush, and the motion of the brush on your gums. Explore the sensations in between the teeth and around the gums while brushing.

The shower is another place to open awareness. Follow the water as it pours out of the shower head and splashes on your face, then as it hits the ground and flows down the drain. What about the light in the shower—is it dim because you are behind a curtain? If so, how does that change the shade of your skin? You probably never noticed, but behind shower curtains, skin tone can indeed look different.

If you use public transportation, examine the details inside buses and trains. Scan to see who's on and where they are sitting. How are the seats arranged? Older buses had the same seating arrangement, two rows of seats, all facing forward. Modern buses arrange seats with more variety. Some seats face inward, some backward, some are single, while others double. Witness these subtle differences. Many public buses also have advertisements. Look at where they are posted and what they say.

Conversations also make for great practice. Pay attention to not only what people say, but how they say it. Are they talking fast or slow, loud or soft? How is their tone? Is there nervousness, anxiety, or anger in their voice, or is it full of excitement and enthusiasm? Does the person appear confident in what he or she is saying or unsure and seeking validation and approval?

These are some ways to pay attention to details. Like retrieval, the exercise doesn't require being in a quiet environment, sitting in a comfortable position, or keeping the eyes closed. It simply requires opening attention and awareness to whatever you are doing and is happening in the moment.

So, you can be at a restaurant, coffee shop, bar, store, park, study hall, library, or bus stop and notice everything, including the seats, tables, people, menu, carpeting, and decorations. Anything and everything. Simply open your eyes, ears, and other senses for details you never noticed or paid attention to before.

This technique is especially useful when waiting, because anytime we are waiting, we are simply twiddling our thumbs, anxious to have the waiting end. Instead of twiddling your thumbs, look around and scan your surroundings. Whether waiting in line, for the train, or for someone to show up, step back and examine finer and finer features and elements in and around the immediate environment.

This technique doesn't require much time and effort—just some practice. As suggested, there are plenty of opportunities to practice. The more you practice, the more attentive you will become and the more easily you can direct attention on what's important.

Examining details is an important component to concentration. Just skimming something or focusing on only one part leads to missing a great deal. As important as the big picture is, details also matter. If you are constantly missing small details and minor but important points, this chapter might be the one to spend time on.

Whether with individual objects or the world at large, perform this exercise regularly and often. It will help you not only get out of your head, but fine tune your ability to narrow in on features that require the utmost scrutiny and patience, and who knows, you may catch things that you missed before.

CHAPTER 8 - PUSHING LIMITS

Everyone has limits on how long they can focus. You may be able to engage in an activity for a few minutes, or even several hours, but eventually can't go further. Attention begins to decline and your mind says stop. If you find it easy to concentrate for short stretches, but get quickly worn out or need prolonged breaks, you have good concentration, you just need to work on extending it.

A great way to do that is by pushing your limits. Just like pushing yourself to do more sit-ups can build and strengthen muscles, pushing yourself to focus builds and strengthens concentration. Doing only what comes easy or stopping when difficulty arises hinders growth. It's pushing for those extra few minutes, even seconds, that make the difference.

Think about marathon runners. Could they run twenty-six miles the first time they laced their running shoes? Of course not. To become marathoners, they pushed beyond their immediate limit. If they could run a mile, they attempted a mile and half, then two. They kept pushing, until over time, they could finish a marathon.

Like many of the techniques and exercises in this book, the concept here is simple. Push your limits on any task, activity, or interaction beyond the moments that are comfortable or easy—or when the desire to stop arises. When the desire arises, instead of stopping that instant, push yourself to go a little further. And then some more. Then a little more.

The following are examples of how to do this:

Reading

If while reading you lose interest or motivation to continue, instead of closing the book, see if you can read one more chapter. If a full chapter is out of reach, go for an additional page. At the end of that page, attempt one more.

When a full page becomes out of reach, aim for one more paragraph. Keep reaching for another paragraph until that too becomes difficult.

At that point, set your sight on additional sentences. Attempt to read the next sentence, then another and another, until you can't anymore. At that point, you can say you've had enough and stop.

Conversation

If you are in a stale conversation or talking to a boring person, stay in it longer than normal. Notice how long you can hang in despite the pain and boredom. If you run out of things to say, see if it's possible to stand in the discomfort of silence.

This may be challenging for those who are not talkative or can't carry a conversation beyond small talk, because once the small talk ends, the immediate response is to end the conversation. You will have to get out of that mode and force a deeper, more meaningful discussion to push the conversation further.

If, on the other hand, you were in a stimulating conversation that, for one reason or another, died, instead of moving on, engage with the person some more. Extend the interaction beyond your natural level of comfort. You might ask a new question, make an extra comment, offer a different opinion, or give additional advice to keep the dialogue going. Push past the immediate discomfort and desire to stop.

Videos

Refrain from skipping boring parts of online videos and shows. If you tend to fast forward through slow, uninteresting, or lackluster moments of YouTube, Netflix, Hulu, or other videos, from now on abstain from that behavior. Push your ability to sit through a video from beginning to end, including the uninteresting parts like the intro.

During those parts, don't let the mind drift. It may help to incorporate the exercise from the previous chapter to notice details you never bothered to notice like the music, camera angle, scenery, or what the actors or characters are wearing.

At times, sitting through the boring parts may be a test of will. You may not be able to hold attention for more than a few seconds. Regardless, do your best. You are building the endurance to expand limits. Even if you can expand it only for a few seconds, it helps. A few seconds now, a few then, and some more next time adds up very quickly.

Breaktime

If you are working on a task or activity and the desire for a break arises, by all means take a break, but don't break in that instant. Refrain for a moment and see how long you can wait. As focus and concentration decline or as frustration builds, will yourself to stay with the work longer. When focus and concentration decline again, muster the strength to go little further.

Material in this Book

Of course, push your limits with the exercises in this book. If an exercise asks you to hold attention for 5 minutes and the longest you can manage is 3, try to rally an additional 10 seconds. Then 10 seconds more. Don't just stop the second you can't go further. Keep attempting to go longer.

These are a few ways to push limits. The advice in this chapter is pure endurance training. The goal is to break through your current limits and build endurance to focus for longer and longer periods.

Though there is a bigger goal than simply building endurance. It's to break the habitual response to ending tasks as soon as the desire to stop arises. That is, habits can be our biggest adversary. Once the body falls into a habituated pattern, it can be difficult to pull it out. As a result, that pattern runs our life. What's more is that anything can become a habit, even the rate you blink your eyes.

If anything can become a habit, so can our response to losing focus when a task becomes difficult. In other words, often we stop a task not because we can't go further, but simply because we've become habituated to stopping. The desire to stop arises and we automatically stop or lose focus.

It's hard to imagine that we lose focus not because we are unable to go further, but solely because the habit is so strong. Unfortunately, that's the power of habits. As amazing and complex as the human body is, this is one of its limitations.

So, the main goal of the advice in this chapter is to break the habitual response to ending a task. This way, you don't automatically lose focus because your desire stopped. By pushing forward despite the pull to stop, you disrupt the habit of succumbing to your inner needs and wants to stop.

This exercise can be practiced on any task or activity. Anytime focus or interest begins to wither, instead of switching to another activity, push further. It doesn't have to be for a long stretch. Aim for just a few more minutes or even seconds.

It helps to practice on activities that you dislike or find boring. I would even suggest seeking out such activities. It's usually these activities that we procrastinate, avoid, and half-ass. Unfortunately, it's also these activities that tend to be the most important, so they require more attention and focus.

Practicing on the boring or unpleasant ensures you can maintain concentration despite your feelings or attitudes toward an activity. You want to get comfortable doing things you dislike. The more you can push to do things you dislike, the longer you can stick with any endeavor.

When starting out, it will be a struggle to push your limits, even for a few extra minutes. Like muscles that have never worked out, your mind likely doesn't yet have the capacity to stay focused on anything in which it has no interest.

Though trust the process. Overtime, the ability will strengthen, and as it does, so will the ability to stay focused down the stretch. And it's down the stretch when focus is most critical.

CHAPTER 9 - IMPULSE CONTROL

The last chapter discussed ways to keep the mind and attention *on* an activity for longer and longer periods by stretching your limits. In this chapter, you will do the opposite. You will keep the mind and attention *away* from an activity by controlling your impulse.

An impulse is a strong and sudden urge to do, say, or behave a certain way. It's an internal force that pushes us to act or react, often without thinking. Impulses make us leap first and think later as there is usually a degree of urgency in the behavior. It is characterized by rapid and unplanned reactions with reduced concern for consequences.

Humans have many impulses such as the impulse to eat, breathe, flee, talk, grab, shop, lie, scratch, give, nourish, mate, fantasize, gamble, conform, lash out, and stand out. Some recent developments include the impulse to check email, surf the web, or scroll through social media.

What's more, impulses drive our behavior. When an impulse arises, we go with it, often without being aware of the action or the decision. How many times has someone told you not to do something, but without thinking, you still did? You went from impulse to action without conscious thought or decision in between.

We are constantly, and unconsciously, acting on impulses. When hungry, we eat. If thirsty, we drink. When anger arises, we lash out. With nervousness, we flee. Where there is boredom, there is YouTube. As notifications ping, we grab the phone. When a fantasy erupts, we drift away. When we see a product, we buy it.

In many ways, concentration is impulse control. It is about refraining from the impulse to jump to another thought, image, feeling, or activity. Anytime you are working, all sorts of impulses will come up. It could be the impulse

71

to call a friend, watch cat videos, use the bathroom, get a glass of water, or even check the front door. Having the impulse in of itself is distracting because another process is competing for the limited space in awareness.

What's worse, these impulses don't show up as light desires. As mentioned, they erupt as a desperate urge to act. The urge can be so strong, it pushes out whatever is in your awareness and makes itself the focal point. You could be writing a report, but the impulse to check email be the only thing on your mind. As you attempt to stick to the report, the impulse's nagging, pestering, and tormenting grows.

What's more, acting on an impulse breaks concentration. The second you open the email app or press *play* on a cat video, concentration is broken. Impulses are the gateway to getting lost in other thoughts, tasks, or activities.

Not only do impulses break concentration, but the mind uses impulses for this exact reason. Yes, the mind is sly and devious. When it doesn't want to engage in an activity, it'll use impulses to pull us away.

It's amazing the number of urges that show up when confronted with an unpleasant task. That is, any time something unpleasant stands before you, a host of impulses will attempt to lure you in a different direction. However, when that assignment is finished or no longer a priority, those urges seem to miraculously vanish. Suddenly, the need to call your mom, sort your socks, or clean the toilet aren't so important.

There are many reasons why the mind pulls us away from a task. It may not like it, find it boring, or too uncomfortable. The mind may also fear making mistakes, being ridiculed for the mistake, or maybe, it simply lacks the motivation in the moment. More importantly, the mind may not *believe* capable of it. Remember from Chapter 3, if an action is not in line with a belief, the mind will keep you from acting. Well, impulses are another way it keeps you from acting.

Also, the mind likes stability and certainty over instability and uncertainty. If the brain thinks, for whatever reason, that what you are doing is risky, too difficult, or dangerous, it will use impulses to pull you in another direction.

Impulses are also how we get caught in a cycle of procrastination. They push and pull us in a million different directions to do a million different things, except the thing we want or need to get done. They shift focus and attention from one avoidance behavior to another.

Often, you won't realize or understand the reasons for the impulse, you'll just feel an insatiable desire to switch gears. You'll think *I'm thirsty, I need a glass of water* or *it's been a while since I've talked to mom, I really should call her*. Next thing you know, the impulse has pulled you away.

The danger of impulses is that they often take over without our conscious awareness. If you remember, impulses have us acting first and thinking later. What this means is an impulse can have you doing something only to realize later that you are doing it.

That is, you might be responding to an important email only to find yourself texting friends. Or one minute you're taking notes in a lecture, the next minute doodling rainbows. That's the power of impulse.

This is where the *what am I doing* or *why did I do that* dialogue shows up. I'm sure you've experienced this on many occasions. You're busy running errands and lose track of what you are doing, so you ask yourself, *what am I doing?* Or you did something you weren't supposed to do only to ponder, *why did I just do that?* Or the big one, *why do I keep doing this!* The answer is that an impulse took over.

Impulse control is an essential life skill. Studies show impulsive people are more likely to procrastinate, indulge, lie, and resort to coping behavior such as overeating. They have a harder time resisting strong emotions like anger, aggression, and fear. Studies also link impulsiveness to higher risks of addictions to cigarettes, alcohol, drugs, gambling, and sex.

Many mental and mood conditions such as Attention Deficit Hyperactivity Disorder (ADHD), Obsessive-Compulsive Disorder (OCD), Bipolar, and Borderline Personality Disorder are associated with high impulsiveness. Even more, those who attempt suicide tend to score higher on impulsivity.

Less impulsive individuals, on the other hand, fare better in life. They have healthier relationships and higher self-esteem while earning advanced degrees and more money. They manage stress better, and overall, less impulsive people tend to be happier. An inverse correlation exists between success and impulsivity, because the ability to subdue a short-term desire leads to long-term gain.

As you can see, impulse control is a big deal. It's what separates us from our primitive ancestors and the rest of the animal kingdom. The ability to control impulses has huge implications, especially on concentration.

Therefore, this chapter will help you develop this critical skill. It will teach you to manage and curb impulses so you can have control over them, instead of them controlling you. By controlling the many impulses in your life, you will have a much easier time controlling the impulses that interfere with concentration.

That means when an impulse to surf the web rears its ugly head while reading, you'll continue reading. If an impulse to pull out the phone creeps in while with family, you'll remain present with family. By refraining from the impulse to daydream in class, you might actually learn something.

Developing Impulse Control

Like pushing limits, impulse control is something you practice throughout the day. It can be practiced on a wide range of tasks, activities, and routines. Since most of our actions originate with an impulse, our days present plenty of opportunities to practice. The following presents the many situations in which to apply this vital skill.

Conversation

A good place to start is in conversation as everyone has to speak to someone at one time or another. Moreover, you may not realize, but much of our impulses arise in conversation. That's because anytime a person says something, we can respond in a variety of ways. All of the varieties create a variety of impulses, for example, to throw out a comment, crack a joke, make a remark, interrupt the person, or have the final word.

The tone in which we respond can also be driven by impulse. We might respond politely even if we feel otherwise or we might respond rudely, even if there is no reason to be rude. Our emotional reactions are too impulsive. Based on what a person says, we may burst into laughter, fall into tears, or erupt with rage without consciously deciding to laugh, cry, or get angry.

To practice, refrain from the many impulses that come up in regular conversation. If you interrupt others in mid-sentence, repress the urge to do that. If you are sarcastic and like to throw out witty remarks, abstain from that too. If you lean toward arguing in conversation, try leaning the other way. If the inclination is to dominate a discussion, step back and allow the other person to lead.

You might even try to pause before responding. Anytime anyone says something, count to 2 before opening your mouth. Now that'll really test your patience.

For a shy person, on the other hand, the natural inclination is not to remark and interrupt. Their compulsion is to refrain and hold back in conversation. Such people may yearn to speak up, but their impulses hold them back. If this is your tendency, for this exercise, practice speaking out. Fight the inclination to withdraw, and instead, speak your mind, express your thoughts and feelings, and disagree with someone's views.

Practicing impulse control in conversation is more difficult than you might imagine. Much of what we say is habitual and automatic. We blurt out comments, statements, and responses without really thinking about them. They just come out.

Despite knowing that much of what you say is habitual and automatic, you may still find it difficult to hold back. It may take sheer will to refrain from expressing what the impulse wants to express. Language is complex, and so is our interaction with another human through language. So, this is as good of a place as any to practice.

Gossip

Human's need for gossip is enormous. Whether it's a celebrity, athlete, next-door neighbor, friend, or foe, we like to know what is happening in people's lives. Not only do we like knowing what people are doing, we love talking to people about it with others. Gossip is often the topic of many conversations, because a juicy gossip is hard to resist.

There seems to be an evolutionary drive to gossip. Knowing what people are doing or not doing has helped us survive by building community, keeping us on the same page, and helping us see who's doing well and who's not. Then, we can use that information to mimic the behaviors of those doing well and avoid the behaviors of those who are not. Gossip also warns us about who might be a possible threat or danger in a group.

Since gossip is an evolutionary drive, it is safe to assume it has a strong impulsive component, making it a great place to practice impulse control. When you have to know what's going on in someone's life, resist the urge to find out. Challenge the temptation to be up on all the latest news, trends, and updates. Test how long you can avoid the longing to know what he said, she did, who's dating who, and what's happening where.

For those who love gossip, this can be a tough impulse to resist. A juicy gossip can be as hard to resist as any other impulse or drive. Often it feels like you must know or you are going to die or lose your mind. These intense moments are the best opportunities to practice resisting impulses. Sit with the temptation and allow yourself to feel the burning sensation of not knowing.

That's the challenge of impulses, they make you feel that way to force you to act. The reality is that you are not going to die or lose your mind. The longer you can sit with the feeling, over time, the less influence it will have on your behavior. Down the road, if an urge to know what someone said or did rises again, you will be able to stay focused on the immediate priority without getting distracted.

Luck and Fortune

Anytime something big happens, like getting a raise or being asked out on a date, there is a strong urge to tell people. Much of our enjoyment from news comes not actually from the news itself, but sharing it with those we love (or with those we may want to make jealous). As touched on in the intro, we are wired to engage and interact with others and sharing good news is part of that.

This provides another opportunity to refrain from impulses. If you stumble upon good fortune, resist the yearning to share it. Fight the urge, even if it takes every ounce of will. Experiment with how long you can withhold the big news before sharing it with the world.

Everyone loves to share news when it is positive, however, how do you handle unpleasant news? Do you get upset, angry, sad, depressed, or quiet? Abstain from your normal or instinctual response to bad news. Receive the negative without exclamation or alarm. Tell yourself *nothing is going to cause me to lose self-control*. This is a form of impulse control too.

In the Car

Most people love listening to the radio while driving. Whether jamming to the latest hits or indulging in talk radio, they enjoy the stimulating sounds hitting their eardrums. If you too love having the radio going, next time you are in the car, see if you can contain the impulse to turn it on. Whether the impulse arises as soon as you hop in or while stuck in traffic, keep your hand from *touching that dial*.

This one requires serious focus because the impulse to engage when driving is intense. Sitting in a car, especially with no one to talk to, gets boring–and fast. Sometimes we need a distraction from our own voice. What you'll discover is that you'll turn on the radio without even realizing. In fact, you might flip through several stations or songs before catching yourself.

When you do, turn the radio off and resist the temptation to turn it back on. Sit with the impulse without acting on it. If your hand reaches for the dial, pull it back. Pay attention to how the hand reaches for the dial without your permission.

Also, notice the pain and frustration of not having any sound or distraction in the car and how it riles you up. There is usually a degree of annoyance or frustration that triggers the impulse. If you can learn to sit through the unpleasantness, you'll be able to sit through the unpleasantness of other impulses.

At the Store

We have all fallen prey to impulsive buying at one time or another. You enter a mall swearing to buy only one item, then poof—you leave with a new shirt, handbag, phone, earrings, and sunglasses. Or you walk into a convenience store to buy a snack, but come out with meals for the week.

This is one of the more common impulsive behaviors. We all like to experience pleasure, joy, and satisfaction, and there are few things in life more pleasurable than buying on impulse. In fact, research suggests the amazing feeling you get when seeing a product plays a decisive role in buying that product.

So, the next time you see a fantastic product that you must have, curb the temptation to have it. Whether it's a stunning dress, fabulous pair of shoes, the latest iPhone, or a new car, resist the impulse to buy it.

If you can't resist the impulse, then at the very least, delay it. Instead of buying the item then and there, wait. Walk around the store before putting the item in the cart. Consider leaving the store for a few hours. Better yet, go home and wait a full day. Maybe a few days. Heck, wait a week. Like the impulse to gossip, sit with the craving without acting on it. You might be surprised to find that the sky won't fall or the world won't end if you don't get it.

Food

Speaking of meals, how do you react when food is in front of you? Do you dig in or are you able to wait? If your standard response is to chow down, try waiting. Though don't wait so long that the food gets cold, just enough to give the impulses a bit of a stir. As you wait, notice how turbulent it feels to restrain the impulse and how the body wants nothing more than to disregard your intention and begin chewing.

Do the same when thirsty. Anytime you reach for a glass of water or a bottle of soda, wait a few minutes longer than usual to start drinking. Again, just a few minutes. The goal is not to dehydrate yourself, but simply to train the body to refrain from an impulse just long enough to have a moment to think before acting. It's all about that moment where you can think before acting that makes all the difference in managing impulses.

You can do this when ordering as well. When you really want to order a particular meal, don't. Order something else. In fact, order the opposite of what the impulse wants. Let the impulsive part know that you won't succumb to it.

Internet

Another great place to practice, especially in this day and age, is online. Cyberspace offers endless opportunities for impulses to arise. So much exists on the internet and so much is calling for attention, that it's easy for the mind to run amuck.

No matter what site you're visiting, almost always there is a link to another page. Whether the link leads to more information about a topic, a similar topic, a different topic, an advertised topic, an advertised product, an internet scam, a newsfeed, a tweet, post, blog, or video—you name it, and there is a link to it. Some sites have so many links and advertisements, it's difficult to find any meaningful content.

Even more, it's much easier to cave in to an impulse online. All it requires is a slight movement of the mouse and a click, and voila, you've caved in. It's so easy, in fact, we mindlessly click away. And this is exactly the way many surf the web, mindlessly clicking from one link to another.

To practice developing restraint online, first start with the impulse to even go online. Consider why you want to surf anyway. Does it serve a work or research purpose? Are you shopping? Maybe the internet just helps kill time, which means there is no immediate need. If there is no need, resist the initial drive to do it.

If there is a purpose, stick with that purpose. With a goal to research, stick with the topic you seek to study. Don't get sidetracked by unrelated articles, reports, or stories. If the intention is to shop, visit only sites that sell the product you seek. Refrain from searches that don't relate to the initial objective, and don't click on that advertisement in the corner for the XJ7000 robot vacuum with the built-in clothe ironing and folding feature.

The biggest draw for our impulses online is the headlines on all the links and advertisements. They are incredibly amazing at luring us in. They build such irresistible curiosity and make such wonderful promises that it's nearly impossible to resist. We've all seen them:

Ten celebrity secrets you never knew, number 7 will shock you!

Click to find out how to get the new iPhone, free!

Where are these child stars now?

The photo that broke the internet!

Know that internet headlines are not put together carelessly. There are entire fields of study around headlines. Every word is crafted to entice the impulsive part of us, which is why we so easily cave in to them. Even though we know from countless experiences that the actual content is never as astounding as the headline suggests, we can't help but click to it.

With that said, be aware of headlines online. When one grabs your attention, pause and ask yourself, *Do I really need to go there? Is the headline just a ploy or will it provide the information I seek?* If you really must click the link, by all means do so, but pause and attempt restraint first. If it is still difficult to resist, close the internet browser and step away from the computer or smartphone for a few minutes.

Curiosity

Curiosity is the biggest driver of impulsive behavior. Humans have an insatiable hunger to know what happened, why it happened, and if it will happen again. It is the reason we gossip, glue ourselves to the news, or spend countless hours online.

To illustrate just how strong this desire is, about 8 years ago, I decided to stop talking about my age. I don't know what motivated the decision, but when people asked, I simply said I don't talk about it. Now, when I used to reveal my age, it was never a big deal. The number passed through people's minds like any other fact, quickly lost in a sea of less important concerns.

Surprisingly, when I stopped revealing my age, people went ballistic. The *curiosity* was too much for them. They couldn't accept the fact that I wouldn't disclose it. Days, weeks, and even months later, many were still hung up about it. It was just a number, but because they didn't know, it created a curiosity they couldn't resist.

Often people did whatever they could to find out. Many of them weren't sneaky or devious, but to find out, they became that way. It was a trip. In fact, it still is a trip. Friends I met years ago are still trying to piece it together. Occasionally, out of the blue, I'll receive a message from them, claiming to have figured it out and how they went about calculating it.

Even more surprising, some would get downright mad and angry, saying things like *that's so stupid, I can't believe you won't say your age.* Again, it wasn't that these people were angry or mean spirited. It was the curiosity.

This is the unrelenting power of curiosity. It creates such an overwhelming impulse, it dominates everything else in our awareness. That's how news, internet, and marketing headlines lure us in. They create a curiosity so grand, it's impossible to ignore.

Despite the impulse curiosity creates, it is nonetheless an extremely valuable trait. Our bottomless wanderlust is the key driver to human exploration and advancement, inspiring us to venture to the furthest reaches of the globe, and even into space.

Like anything in life, though, too much curiosity becomes the opposite. It becomes a hindrance to personal growth, productivity, and of course, concentration. Spending all our time chasing celebrity gossip, reading internet articles, watching the news, or following the score leaves less time for anything else. The insatiable hunger to know turns into a distraction that pulls us away from what we truly need or want to be doing. The more we seek, the further away we are pulled.

At some point, you have to say *enough* and tell yourself *I don't need to be in the loop on every juicy detail or scientific fact. I just want to pay attention to this task and finish it to the best of my abilities, so I can enjoy the present moment.* Once you arrive at this point, you are truly ready to start your concentration training.

Whatever piques your curiosity, resist its pull. Resist the draw to know which team won the game last night. Shake the need to see what all the commotion is about. If you see a magic trick, let go of wanting to know how it was done. When meeting someone new, see how long you can carry the interaction before asking their age or profession.

To make it easier to manage curiosity's impulsive grip, know that curiosity never ends.

NEVER!

As soon we answer one question, another question appears. In fact, knowing more doesn't satisfy our hunger, it only makes us more hungry. The more we know, the more we want to know, leaving only a momentary respite between answers.

So curbing curiosity is a big step towards impulse control as the majority of our impulsive drives are triggered by curiosity. Developing restraint in this area keeps us from fixating on captivating news stories or seductive headlines that make big promises, but leave little to be had.

Now I'm not saying, never watch the news or go online. That's not the goal of these exercises. The goal is to be aware of the decision to act and to act purposefully–when you want, and not when they get in the way of other priorities.

These are a few ways to practice impulse control. As mentioned, the exercise can be practiced anytime, anywhere, and on just about any activity. Whenever you have an impulsive or habituated response to a person, place, event, circumstance, or outcome, the opportunity to practice exists. For instance, after a YouTube video ends, resist the urge to click on the next video the site recommends. If a notification goes off, deny the temptation to check it.

Though impulse control is no walk in the park. It requires considerable focus and intention, and at times, can be grueling, strenuous, and back breakingly difficult. Chances are you'll need to work on this area over an extended period where progress is several steps forward and several steps back.

In addition to being tough, this one is painful, more painful than any of the other exercises presented so far. The previous exercises are designed to develop mental control so they revolve around training the mind.

This one has a more physical component. You are not just resisting the mind, but the body. Impulses drive us to act, so by resisting an impulse, you are in effect resisting a physical action.

Repressing a physical action can result in considerable physical discomfort and pain as the muscles are pushed and pulled in opposing directions. This physical component adds to the challenge of impulse control.

Another element to highlight is that when you first refrain from an impulse, the desire doesn't initially subside, it grows. Said differently, resisting an impulse initially makes it stronger.

It's like Newton's third law of motion, *for every action, there is an equal and opposite reaction.* When we force something to happen, our internal mechanisms resist with an equal and opposite force. That is, our impulse fights back equally hard.

Remember that an impulse is a strong and sudden desire to act. Like our emotions, the desire is there for a purpose. It wants to act. By holding back that desire, you are keeping it from doing what it is built to do. That's why the desire grows stronger, to summon the strength to complete what it believes is necessary. The more you restrain this desire, the stronger it gets.

As a result, the first few attempts at controlling an impulse may be the most challenging thing you ever do. It will feel like pulling teeth, and that's if you are lucky. At times, you will have to muster every ounce of will from every corner of your being to hold back. And your efforts may last only a few seconds.

When this happens, it is easy to assume that it will always be like this–that every action will be met with this level of strong and overwhelming resistance. It's important to realize the push back is only this strong in the beginning stages. As strides are made to stand up to impulses, they weaken and become easier to resist. The body learns that it's not okay to act on impulses and that any attempts will be met with challenge.

Also, as briefly eluded, the goal of these exercises is not to suppress the impulse, but to delay it. If you can delay for even a few seconds, you give yourself just enough time to think before acting. This goes a long way in one's ability to control an impulse that may divert perfectly good concentration.

Too often we engage in impulses simply because they come up, not realizing that we are acting on them or blindly assuming we made the choice to act. Rather than acting unknowingly or unwillingly, you can evaluate an alternative course, so that you might avoid doing something which you have no desire to do in the first place.

Overtime, such efforts build on themselves. Each time an impulse is delayed, it's a step in delaying it further. Then the next time, attempt to delay it even further. Bear Bryant, 25-year coach at the University of Alabama, says, *The first time you quit, it's hard. The second time, it gets easier. The third time, you don't even have to think about it.* Impulse control works the same. The practice builds over time, not in one go.

Nonetheless, impulses have the uncanny ability to convince us that if we don't act, the outcome will be catastrophic. That's how they compel us to act. With practice, you will realize the world will not end if an impulse is ignored. You and your body will learn that it's okay if an impulse is not met. In fact, it's more than okay. This will make further attempts easier. Remember, just because an impulse arises doesn't mean you have to act on it!

To aid your efforts, it helps to understand how impulses arise or take over. Usually, a person feels increasing tension or arousal before the action. The growing tension can be so painful, one is left with no choice but to act, just to remove the pain. Often the arousal and action are simultaneous. You will have a strong desire to act and are simultaneously acting.

Furthermore, research shows that self-control is harder to sustain as the day progresses. That's because impulse control requires energy and motivation, and sometimes a lot. Later in the day, we tend to have less of both, increasing the likelihood of caving in to them. Just because your *will* feels invincible in the morning, it may not last through to the evening.

Since both energy and will decline over the course of the day, that means impulse control is a game of balance. The trick is to not burn out too early, but instead, pace energy and motivation through the day. Keep an eye on the fuel gauge and make sure there is plenty in reserve. It doesn't serve to control impulses in the beginning of the day only to give in to them by the end. Without building balance into the plan, even the fiercest explosion of *will* is not sustainable.

The exercises in this chapter prove the point that much of what we do is outside our conscious control. By practicing impulse control, you'll clearly see that most of what you do is just happening. You have the illusion that you are in control, but the reality is, your unconscious mechanisms are running the show. This is what people mean when they talk about self-control—the ability to resist our unconscious drives, needs, and impulses to act and behave in healthy, productive ways.

If you notice, this chapter spends more time on a single technique than any other chapter in the book. That's because impulse control is critical to concentration. As stated, impulse control is concentration. It is the ability to repress all the relentless urges and drives that surface when trying to focus. As you've learned throughout the book, the human mind and body can swing in a million different directions. That's how we're built. The ability to restrain these swings is vital for concentration

The people who naturally have strong concentration are those who naturally have less swings. Impulses don't arise as often and frequently for them, so their lives aren't a constant battle of resisting one stimulus after another. Since impulses aren't pulling their attention, they remain focused.

Unfortunately, most of us are not as gifted, which means we need to put effort in this area. The exercises in this chapter are designed for this purpose. They will help you develop the awareness to **know** when an impulse is arising and the ability to **pause** before acting.

As noted several times, it's really all about this pause. Like with pushing limits, there is a bigger goal to the exercises in this chapter. That goal is to develop the habit to pause when an impulse arises. This *pause* gives you the space to think before acting. When you can think before an action, you can make rational and constructive choices.

Best of all, impulse control is a highly transferable skill. Developing control in one area of life carries over to other areas, including concentration. That pause ingrains as a habit that instantly kicks in whenever an impulse arises, giving you time to think before acting.

Over time, avoiding interruptions and diversions will become second nature. Any time an impulse arises, you pause, which gives you a moment to think. From there, you can either continue doing what you were doing or make a conscious decision to do something else.

With that said, if you are serious about developing concentration, in addition to self-talk, take the advice in this chapter to heart and practice impulse control and practice it in all areas of life.

CHAPTER 10 - TRAINING THE BODY

Humans, like most animals, are built to be in motion. We are constantly and endlessly moving or doing something, even when sitting or lying down. Either we are biting our nails, licking our lips, twirling our hair, scratching our head, bouncing our leg, or tapping our feet. You name it and we are moving in one way or another.

What's more, the body needs to be moving and engaged. This is the reason sitting on a bus or plane for an extended period is so difficult or why boredom so painful. This also explains why many drink alcohol to relax or smoke weed to *chill*. It's as if the only way to keep the body still is to sedate it. Even during sleep, it is said we toss and turn as much as 20 times per hour.

Like the majority of what's happening inside, most of these movements are unconscious. We don't choose to do them; they happen on their own. Often, we are not aware of them, even in the act. Words like *tic, twitch, jerk, fidget, jitter, shiver, quiver, tremble, shake* and *spasm* all describe movements the body makes without our conscious choice.

That means the physical body can hinder concentration as much as anything else. If you can't stop moving, adjusting, fidgeting, or can't keep your body under control in other ways, it will interfere with whatever you hope to accomplish. It's hard to believe, but your own body can become a distraction.

Distractions from the body manifest in many ways. They arise from movements as previously described, but also from fiddling with one's clothes or hair, playing with objects such as pens, rings, or glasses, doodling rainbows instead of taking notes, or constantly changing positions when sitting.

As you will learn in the next section, sometimes these movements can aid concentration as they preoccupy a part of the mind and body that needs stimulation. In general, physical movements create hurdles that lead to poor learning and memory.

In fact, studies reveal that unconscious movements like fidgeting or playing with one's hair are signs that concentration is lost. They usually occur when the mind is spaced out. So, if you catch yourself fidgeting or in any of the previously mentioned unconscious movements, it's a clue that you've, on one or more levels, disengaged and are running on autopilot.

Even more, growing body of literature reveals that developing control over physical movements is necessary for improving attention and concentration. A 2015 study of mindful movement and skilled attention by Dav Clark, Frank Schumann, and Stewart Mostofsky stated *that the process of controlling attentional movement cannot be cleanly separated from the selection of physical movements.* In other words, motor control is the key to mind control.

Since the body can get in the way of concentration, this chapter explores ways to develop motor control. It offers three exercises that train the body to work with the mind in concentration. The first exercise develops control over involuntary muscle movements. The second exercise advances the ability to fully concentrate on—and gain conscious control of—each move you make. The last promotes focus while moving physically.

Together these exercises bring consciousness to your actions and acute awareness of your involuntary movements. Self-awareness is the first step to self-control, and over time, such awareness will provide greater discipline and restraint throughout the day. These exercises will be especially useful to those whose work requires physical activity.

Exercise 1 - Head Turn

This exercise can be done standing or sitting. Fix your eyes on a spot straight ahead. The spot could be an object or even a small dot on the wall.

Open your arms out to the sides so you look like the letter *t*.

Keeping your gaze ahead, turn your head to the right. Then turn it to the left. Continue the motion of turning your head right to left and left to right for a total of 10 times.

Make sure only your head moves, not the eyes. The eyes should always be looking ahead.

In addition to looking ahead, keep the arms and body steady. Refrain from moving the arms up and down or side to side, and keep the body from swaying in any way. Simply stay as still as possible.

This exercise does two things. First, it develops resistance to involuntary muscle movements. Second, it trains the body to stay still in a difficult position with hands held out.

More importantly, it trains concentration to keep focus in front of you. No matter what is going on with the body, the eyes are looking straight. So, if you begin scratching your head in confusion while reading, your eyes remain on the page. If you're twiddling a pen in a lecture, your eyes remain on the speaker. If you're multitasking while talking, the eyes stay with the person with whom you're talking.

Exercise 2 - Fist and Arm Curl

While sitting in front of a table, put your arms on the table with the backs of your hands facing down. Make a fist with your thumb across the top of your fingers.

While paying close attention, slowly uncurl each of your fingers. First uncurl the thumb, then the index finger, then the middle finger, and so on until the hand is fully open.

Once the hand is open, curl the fingers back into a fist, drawing in the pinky first, then the rest of the fingers in succession until the thumb is back over the fist.

Still concentrating on each movement, lift your fist off the table and curl your arm until your fist touches the shoulder. Slowly lower your arm until the back of the hand touches the table again.

Do this first with the right arm, then with the left.

Remember to keep attention on every movement from the fingers folding and unfolding to the arms curling and uncurling. This is the key to the exercise, otherwise, you're just unconsciously moving your hands.

Exercise 3 - Walking Concentration

It's difficult to pay attention to repetitive movements, because over time, repetitive movements become habits that can be performed without thinking about or being aware of them. As you can imagine, this can be beneficial as it allows you to do one thing while thinking about something else.

In some ways, though, it can be harmful. Certain jobs, no matter how repetitive, require strict concentration to catch discrepancies, avoid problems, or prevent injuries.

This exercise trains you to remain aware in such repetitive endeavors. It requires taking the most repetitive activity, which for humans is walking, and then counting each step using a sequence that requires deliberate thought.

While walking, count 5 steps (1, 2, 3, 4, 5).

After the fifth step, start at 2 and count 5 more steps, but this time by every other number (2, 4, 6, 8, 10).

Next start at 3 and count 5 steps again, but back to every number (3, 4, 5, 6, 7).

Then start at 4 and count 5 steps every other number (4, 6, 8, 10, 12).

Keep counting 5 steps, but each time you reach the fifth step, restart 1 number higher than the previous round and switch between counting by every number to every other number.

Does this seem confusing?

That's the point!

The sequence prevents you from counting simply by habit. You have to know the number you are on, how many steps to go before restarting, and whether to count every number or every other number. And since the starting number changes each round, the sequence keeps changing.

If this seems challenging now, imagine the focus needed to do this while walking. It will be impossible to think about anything else even though you are performing the exercise on a deeply habitual activity like walking. This exercise is particularly useful for people who do repetitive work.

This sums up the three exercises on training the body. As you learned, the body not only needs to move, but it is built to move. It is moving in all ways always.

I want to share a secret to change your perspective on concentration, and even on work, especially work you dislike. Since the body is built to move and it needs to move and be engaged, the next time you don't want to do something, think about what else you would do? If you don't engage in the immediate task, what is the other option?

You can't not do nothing!

That's not how we are built.

As humans, we always need to be doing something, whether it's watching T.V., having a drink, or listening to music. No one ever just sits there doing nothing–ever! That's why shortly after retirement, many find another job to fill their time. Although you may not want to do what you are doing currently, what you'll do instead is find some other activity to preoccupy your mind and body.

The point is, if you must be engaged in an activity, why not just engage in the activity that you initially set out to do? Sure, certain activities are nourishing and certain we enjoy. But often, much of what we do is to preoccupy our mind and body's innate need to be preoccupied. If you are going to preoccupy yourself with something, might as well start with what you need to do instead of things that procrastinate you from life.

Selecting the Exercises

This ends the section on concentration training.

There you go, over a dozen exercises to boost, strengthen, and invigorate focus.

As promised, this section went deep. The purpose was to rewire the mind and body so you are naturally more attentive, instead of constantly wrestling to stay on the straight and narrow.

As stressed several times, doing so requires time, effort, and work and it's not always glamorous. In fact, it's rarely glamorous. This is why this book does not fill you with motivational pep-talk or paint a life of excitement and fun.

It's easy to craft writing to make any chore sound sexy, joyous, and oh so exciting. Such writing might motivate you to start, but shortly after starting, you'll hit the walls of your inner mechanisms and realize work takes work.

In fact, work is rarely as desirable as it is made to seem. That's why my books don't focus on feel good advice that simply pump you with feel good emotions. Nor do I spend time on long, drawn out introductions with stories of my life and the endless possibilities of achievement.

Although I'll talk more about my story and the journey that lead to writing this book later, don't get lost in the stories. If you want the motivational, feel good advice, there are million and one books with that. If you want practicable tips that create lasting change, it begins with applying the techniques and doing exercises in this section.

Let's summarize all the exercises in this section.

- **Chapter 3** taught you self-talk and to create a set of statements that describe the changes you desire in this area and to affirm each statement 10 times daily.

- **Chapter 4** introduced three visualization exercises. The first trained you to hold an image, the next to manipulate that image, and the last to see yourself concentrating to the best of your abilities.

- **Chapter 5** also presented three exercises, but to manage your inner thoughts, images, and feelings. It began with learning to ignore them, then clear them from mind, and lastly, to notice them.

- **Chapter 6** introduced the idea that many people are so distracted by the outside world, they can't follow their own thoughts. To combat this, it offered retrieval, a technique that also enhances memory.

- **Chapter 7** addresses the opposite problem, those who are so trapped in their head, they miss what's happening around them. The exercise involved paying attention to detail.

- **Chapter 8** stretched your ability to concentrate by pushing your limits.

- **Chapter 9** did the opposite by training you to keep the mind and attention *away* from an activity through impulse control.

- **Chapter 10** used motor control to develop mind control.

Although you have over a dozen exercises at your disposal, it's best not to practice all of them at once. For one, not all the exercises work together. Second, it's difficult to remember what to do, much less to do it, when trying to do everything. Lastly, attempting all the exercises at once will only lead to confusion, not concentration.

Instead, select one or two exercises and stick with them until you become familiar enough to do on your own and begin to see improvements. Ironically, this poses a challenge for people who lack focus since their natural tendency is to jump from one thing to another. Sticking to an exercise will be an exercise in concentration in of itself.

To select the best exercise, think about the areas that present the most struggle, then identify the chapter or chapters that address that problem. If your challenge lies with controlling inner thoughts, the techniques in Chapters 3, 4, and 5 will prove useful. If your struggles stem from resisting impulses, Chapter 9 on impulse control is the ticket.

After identifying the chapters, evaluate the exercises within those chapters. Pick a few that you can remember, won't take much effort, or something you feel comfortable doing. Focus only on those techniques for several weeks. Work them into your daily routine and do them every day, or *at the very least*, every other day.

Consistency is key.

These exercises are not about how hard you work, but how consistent you are in your efforts. Doing them here and there will provide little value. Everything in life requires frequent and consistent use to realize results.

To remain consistent, it's important to have a plan. When will you do them, where, and for how long? If you don't have a plan, but just say, *I'll do them when I think of it,* you likely won't think of it often and won't do them regularly enough to make an impact.

So, pick a time that you will have each day to practice. You might take the first five minutes of your break, a few minutes just before bed, or any other time that fits into your routine. Also, it helps to pick moments of the day when you are typically energetic and awake.

Set an alarm on the phone or leave a reminder on the bedpost, refrigerator, or desk so you don't forget to practice. Over time, the practice will become routine and you will no longer need reminders.

After mastering one exercise, move to another. Keep working the exercises and building more and more skill.

Before moving to the next section, if you like what you've been learning and find it informative and useful, please take a minute to leave a positive review where you made the purchase. Your time, effort, and opinion matter and help tremendously in getting the word out about this life-important skill.

SECTION III – IN THE MOMENT TOOLS

CHAPTER 11 - STATE CONTROL

So, you've been practicing the exercises in the previous section, increasing awareness of your inner thoughts, images, and feelings, and taking healthy steps to develop new and better habits. Gradually, the ability to hold attention for longer and longer periods is developing.

Still, your thoughts buzz like errand bees, flying in every direction, but never landing long enough to accomplish anything. The harder you try, the more elusive attention becomes. You stare into empty space, daydreaming while the task, assignment, or exam waits in front of you, unfinished.

The exercises in the last section are great for developing concentration over the long term, though often, situations call for a boost in the moment. Either you've got an assignment due tomorrow, report to hand in next week, or worse, a deadline to meet in a few hours. Therefore, you need a way to sharpen focus and fast.

The chapters in this section present simple, yet extraordinarily effective tools that boost attention to push through immediate hurdles and goals. These tools create internal shifts that can give momentary reprieve from a distracted mind.

The section starts with a tool designed to calm your mental, emotional, and physical state. As you've been learning, tremendous commotion resides inside the mind and body. In addition to thoughts, images, and feelings, you have impulses, drives, and bodily movements, all of which interfere with concentration.

As you've also been learning, these things aren't easy to silence. You can't tell the mind to stop racing and you can't always ignore an emotion, especially an overpowering one. It takes time, effort, and training to manage these things. Buddhist monks spend their entire lives in this endeavor.

Fortunately, there is one trick that offers immediate respite without the need to spend years in an ashram. That trick is *relaxation*. To calm the mind, it helps to calm yourself, and the easiest way to do that is through deliberate relaxation.

Relaxing influences your entire state. It not only puts the brakes on the mind, but also sedates the body and impulses from springing in every direction. More importantly, relaxation dampens the emotions so you are not bouncing from one erratic feeling to another.

All of this happens naturally. There is no need to struggle or force yourself to resist an impulse, ignore a feeling, or clear a thought, as they don't arise or nearly as strong. You just work on calming yourself and the rest takes care of itself.

When the volume of your thoughts and emotions are turned downed, you'll be surprised just how easy it is to think, hold a thought, and well, concentrate. You'll find ideas flow easily and naturally, with little strain or effort.

To experience the effects of relaxation, here is a script to get started:

1. Find a comfortable place free from distractions. Close your eyes and take note of what is going on internally. What is your breath like—is it short and shallow or long and deep? Observe your thoughts—how are they moving and what are you thinking?

2. Dive below the thoughts and bring your emotions into awareness. Are they of sadness, nervousness, anger, joy, or a mix? Dive further and observe the sensations in the body. Is there tightness in the muscles, stiffness in the joints, or tension anywhere else? Don't try to change, rationalize, manipulate, or resist these things. Simply observe.

3. Turn attention back to the breath and begin taking deeper breaths. Inhale through the nose while counting to 3–hold for 1 second–then exhale through the mouth while counting to 3. Make sure each inhale is through the nose as the body absorbs oxygen better from the nasal passage. Oxygen both calms the mind and energizes the

body, so deep breaths in through the nose has both a calming and energizing effect.

Keep attention on the breath. With each inhale, witness the air flowing into the lungs, then with each exhale, witness the air flowing out. Heed only the movement of air in and out.

4. Notice where you have tension or pain and attempt to unwind and relax those areas. Scan the neck, shoulders, arms, hands, fingers, hips, thighs, calves, feet, and toes. If you believe that it's not possible to relax an area because pain has always been there, try anyway.

5. Next, add the element of visualization. With the eyes still closed, picture a soothing scene like snowcapped mountains, lush forest, or a sunny beach. Fix the image clearly in mind.

Now, insert yourself into that image. Imagine that you're there experiencing everything with your senses. See the trees swaying in the wind or the grass wrestling in the breeze, hear the waves of the ocean or the fall of rain, smell the scent of the sea or coconuts in the trees, feel the coolness of the air or the sun's rays hitting your skin.

6. As you imagine the scene, repeat the mantra, *I am calm and relaxed.* Say it loud enough to hear, however, if you are in an environment where you can't or don't want to be loud, in your head is fine. Repeat the mantra several times, in succession, as you relax the muscles into a still and gentle state.

Abstain from rushing through the exercise. The goal is to slow down, so any attempt to rush hinders the process. You can add relaxing music, if you wish, or the tranquil sounds of nature.

How do you feel?

There is likely a sense of calmness and control. You're not restless, agitated, or stirred. Nor is there a push to go somewhere, jump to something, or a pull from someplace.

It's easy to see why relaxation works so well. The effects are immediate, without the need to put in enormous time, effort, or mental strain. Anytime you find it difficult to command awareness, take a minute to calm down with this exercise.

You'll find that a looming deadline or the sheer quantity of work in front of you doesn't elicit the strong emotions of stress or overwhelm. Those emotions, consequently, don't incite thoughts of worry or images of what might happen if the deadline is missed. Again, once these automatic processes are slowed, it becomes easier to think, hold a thought, and well, concentrate.

This section began with relaxation because it is a great in the moment tool. Anytime you find yourself distracted and unable to steer away from the distraction, close your eyes and breathe deeply for a few minutes. It will do wonders to push the madness away.

This exercise not only sparks concentration in the moment, but is designed to build concentration over time. If you notice, the instructions ask you to *observe* what is going on inside, *pay attention* to the breath, *visualize* mental images, and repeat a *self-talk* mantra—all exercises presented in the previous section.

Spending a few minutes, few times a day relaxing the mind and body can bring the inner peace to confidently face the world. It can even save your life, as such exercises are known to reduce blockages in blood vessels and lower the risk of heart attack and stroke. Finding those few minutes can seem out of reach, though over time, you may begin to look forward to these tiny vacations from the world.

CHAPTER 12 - DIRECTED QUESTIONS

Did you know, there is a mechanism in your mind designed to seek answers whenever a question is asked. That is, anytime the mind hears a question, whether asked by you or someone else, a mental process is triggered that begins seeking possible answers.

This mechanism is automatic. You don't control it, it just happens. And you can't really stop it either. When a question is asked, the mechanism is triggered, and answers are sought.

Often, it doesn't matter how rational the question is, the mechanism of the mind simply begins searching for possible solutions and answers, and then brings those solutions and answers into your awareness.

That means you can ask two opposing questions and this mechanism will seek answers to both. For example, you might ask yourself, *why are kids so annoying*? The mechanism might come up with answers like, *they are loud, they don't listen*, or that *they are out of control*.

Now consider asking the opposite question, *why are kids so fun?* The responses will be totally different. They will be in line with the fun qualities of kids like *they are innocent, playful*, and *full of joy and energy*.

Whether you truly think kids are annoying or fun is irrelevant. The answers your mind gives will be directly in line with the question that you asked.

This is happening all the time, all around you. You might be watching a tragic story on the news and blurt out *how could that happen*, with the person beside you suggesting a likely reason. Or you might be venting about *how a coworker could be so mean,* with another co-worker offering a possible explanation. Again, this happens because questions activate this answer-seeking mechanism.

Since asking questions engages the mind, this is a great way to engage concentration. You can do so by asking questions about how to improve or direct concentration. You might ask yourself, *how can I be more focused, how can I be aware of what I am doing,* or *in what ways can I improve concentration?* Asking such questions disengages everything going on in the mind and redirects it to seek answers to these questions.

Not only will your mind seek answers on how to be more attentive, but it will automatically make you more attentive. That's because questions signal to the brain that you seek that outcome, so it will do its best to achieve that outcome.

In this case, the questions signal that you seek to pay attention and so the brain will do its best to make you attentive. It will even take the suggestions it comes up with and automatically put them into practice.

There are two ways to apply Directed Questions.

1. Each morning, start your day by asking a few simple questions that direct your mind to concentrate better. You can ask yourself *How can I stay focused on everything I have to do today? How can I be more present and attentive when I am doing those things?* As I mentioned, asking directs the mind to figure out how, and at the same time, make it happen.

You can continue the questioning throughout the day as needed. If around mid-day, your mind starts to wander or you begin to get lost in unrelated thoughts, you can say *my concentration was good this morning, how can I keep it up through the afternoon? What can I do to remain in the here and now? or How can I continue to enhance my focus of present experiences?* This will help you remain focused throughout the day.

2. The other way is to ask questions relevant to specific situations and tasks. Let's say you are conversing with your boss, but your mind is everywhere but on his words. Silently ask, *what is this person saying, what is he or she trying to communicate,* or you might ask *what does this person want me to know and why?* To answer these questions, your brain needs to pay attention to what the person is saying, and so it will start paying attention. This will make you more engaged in the conversation and more aware of what is being said.

In another scenario, let's say you're reading a report or a book, but find you are unable to take anything in. You have gone through pages and pages of text, but nothing has registered. In such moments, ask, *how can I read this chapter or article with full focus and attention* or *how can I spend the next 30 minutes fully engaged in this material?* You might even ask yourself what the contents of this book or article is about or why it is important. Again, doing so will trigger your answer seeking mechanism to seek answers. The way for it to arrive at the answer is to pay attention to what you're reading, thus making you more attentive to what you're reading.

To summarize, anytime focus is lost, ask a few simple questions to direct it back to the activity. If you are not immediately engaged in the task, wait a few moments. Review the answers that surface, and if they offer a solution, follow it. An advice that may emerge is *put away your phone*, so then put it away. Another suggestion might advise *open the book and start reading*, so open the book and start reading.

It sounds simple, but sometimes your unconscious must arrive at the solution for you to be able to act on it. As you've learned, if the unconscious wants to prevent you from acting, it can. So, to act, the unconscious must open the gates to action. It is more inclined to open the gates if it comes up with the solution. Posing these questions in a way tricks the mind to open the gates to focus.

I like to make it as easy as possible to use a technique. So, here are additional done-for-you questions you can ask yourself to stay engaged:

When briefed on a new project, ask, *what is my role, with whom will I need to coordinate, how long will this project last,* and *what is the aim of the project?* The mind will have to pay attention to get at these answers.

When reading a personal development book, inquire, *what three ways can I apply the lessons to my life? How do they know that X is true? Why does Y happen?* Or if you had the chance to meet the author, what would you ask him or her instead of reading the book?

Before walking into a lecture, pose, *I wonder what I will learn today, how will this fit with what I already know or with the previous material,* or *how will this relate to what is on the exam next week?*

It helps to think about your goal for reading the book, going to class, doing the assignments, studying for the exam, or attending the meeting, and then, rephrase the goal into a question. For instance, if your goal for reading a photography book is to improve your landscape shots, you can ask, *how can I use the information in this book to improve my landscape photography?* While reading, the mind will pay attention to and think about ways the information can be applied to enhance that skill.

The only challenge with this technique is that it's hard to know how long the boost to concentration will last. Posing a question might redirect the mind for a few minutes or through an entire meeting. If the boost is short lived, ask the question again and keep doing so until the activity is complete. Certain activities require frequent use of directed questions to remain engaged to the end.

CHAPTER 13 - WHAT'S YOUR GOAL

Ever notice how difficult it is to focus on anything but food when hungry. Thoughts of eating consume your entire awareness so nothing else can enter. It is difficult to think even on pressing matters. As each second passes, the craving grows and grows, and before long, you are fantasizing, even romanticizing, about eating. You can't wait until the luscious, savory taste of the next meal hits your tongue.

Now think about the last time you wanted something really bad, like the latest iPhone, newest game console, the championship trophy, or even a high-rise condominium in the city. Recall how that too consumed your awareness, making it impossible to think about anything or anyone else. You couldn't care about what you already owned or was going right in life as your entire attention was on the object of your desire.

Parents understand this heightened sense of attention all too well. Imagine losing a child in a mall or at an outdoor event. You are frantic, running around, feverishly searching all corners of the venue. Whatever you went into the mall to buy is hardly a concern. What's important is the *goal* of finding your loved one.

All three examples illustrate one thing—the mind is a goal driven and target seeking machine. Goals, objectives, and targets create a magical shift that rearrange priorities and focus. The mind could be thinking about a host of trivial matters, but as soon as a goal is presented, all that is pushed aside. Suddenly, you are not wandering or distracted, but rather focused and occupied on the objective.

The keywords in the last sentence are that you are not *wandering, distracted*, and instead, *focused*. That means setting goals naturally elevates focus. With a precise target of what you want, all sorts of forces, like motivation, enthusiasm, and energy, shift and center around that specific aim. Thoughts, feelings, and impulses even change. Instead of firing to pull you away from the goal, they fire in ways to push you towards it.

That's why during hunger, instead of fantasizing about that dream car, you are fantasizing about a savory steak. With the prospect of a new toy, instead of being angry about what happened yesterday, you are thrilled and excited for what's to come. Even your view changes. You might think being disruptive in class is fun, but with a goal of acing an exam, all that changes. Without effort, you vibrate on a different frequency.

Since goals have the magical ability to channel energy and vibrate you on a different frequency, they obviously make for a great tool to aid concentration. When concentration is lost, set a goal to align the unconscious mechanisms with the conscious desire. State a clear intention of the outcome.

In other words, figure out what you seek to achieve. What is it that you aspire to get out of the task or assignment on which you are so desperately trying to concentrate? In short, what is the end goal?

Is it to ace an exam, write a killer proposal, attract a new client, engage with your spouse, be present with the kids, fix the faucet, or prepare for a successful meeting with the boss? Whatever you seek, clearly state it.

Without a clear objective, the tendency for the mind is to half-ass everything, instead of putting its effort in any one direction. Worse, it sits there doing nothing, which might explain why you are sitting there unable to get started or make worthwhile progress.

Having said that, the next time you find yourself trying to get a grip on concentration, take a step back and set a goal. Decide what you want to get out of the time and why? The goal does not have to be long, drawn out, or complicated. It can be as simple as *My goal is to read 10 pages of Chapter 10 to ace the history exam.*

Although the goal needn't be drawn out, it does need to be specific. And not just about what you are trying to do, but the outcome you seek. Don't merely state that you seek to *finish the assignment*, say *I seek to write an English paper that will get an A*. Or, instead of setting a goal to *develop a killer business proposal*, set a goal to *develop a proposal the client can't refuse.* Include both what you need to *do* and the *outcome* you desire. Both are vital.

As straightforward as this suggestion is, you might find it annoying to set a purpose and always have to do so when focus is running low. That's because it takes effort to put into words what you already know or think your mind should know. Often, it's easier to keep straining on the assignment, then to step back for a minute to define an outcome.

As mentioned in the last chapter, I like to make it as easy as possible to apply a technique. So, below are some sample goals. They present possible situations you may find yourself stuck in and a possible goal you can state to get yourself out. Anytime you are stuck, modify one of these goals to your situation and state it aloud or in your mind.

- *Read chapter 10 of the novel to answer all the quiz questions correctly.*

- *Gather all the receipts and file expenses by the end of the day.*

- *Review notes, practice exams, and assignments to earn a B or better grade on the math midterm.*

- *Write an inspiring social media post that will get at least 50 likes and 10 comments.*

- *List all the supplies I need to buy and order them online for delivery by Friday.*

- *Prepare a presentation that prospective clients will find professional and informative.*

- *Edit article so it is compelling enough to be accepted into publication.*

- *Call mom to catch up on her week.*

- *Check up on brothers and sisters to see if they need anything.*

- *Brainstorm solutions the customer will like.*

- *Plan an exciting vacation to the Bahamas that involves sunbathing, swimming, and scuba diving that will cost under $2,000.*

- *Reach out to Nereida to schedule a lunch date.*

- *Write a clear and detailed proposal of the required changes.*

- *Prepare for Wednesday's meeting with the boss that highlights my knowledge and skills on the issue.*

- *Write a detailed grocery list for the week.*

- *Run all the errands on my plate by the end of the day / week / weekend.*

- *Research where to buy the best running shoes at the lowest price.*

- *Develop clear instructions for staff to follow.*

Again, it's easy to get stuck trying to think about a purpose and phrasing it correctly, and instead of coming up with something, evade the tool completely. Rather than evade the suggestion, take the sample goals here, modify it to your situation, and repeat it to yourself or aloud. The simple declaration can shuffle inner priorities and do wonders for concentration.

CHAPTER 14 - TO DO OR NOT TO DO

I hope you're starting to see that there is quite a lot of activity inside your mind and body. As stated, all this activity is not there for the sake of being there. They are there to warn, guide, and assist as you move about the world. One of the ways they do that is by reminding you of things you should be doing or need to get done.

For instance, you might be on the phone, and out of nowhere, get a twinge of fear signaling that you left the oven on. Or you might be driving, and out of nowhere, a thought pops up reminding you to pick up the laundry. At any given moment, the unconscious is tracking all sorts of tasks you should be doing or need to get done, and throughout the day, reminding you about them.

The problem is, when you track too many things in your head, the mind gets overloaded. There is too much for it to keep straight. This impedes concentration, because instead of using the resources of the mind to focus on a task, the resources are being used to track a bunch of reminders.

In other words, awareness fills up with so many reminders that no room is left for anything else. All the mind's processing power is allocated to remembering to get everything done, but nothing left over to actually get anything done.

What's worse, having too many reminders to track causes worry, anxiety, and fear to build because now the mind is unsure if you'll remember everything, or worse, have enough time to finish it all. Now, the head is not only filled with reminders, but also with worries about whether the reminders will be completed.

This adds to the challenge of concentrating, because as soon as you sit down to do one task, your head bubbles with thoughts of *wait, what about this, don't forget that, if I start here, how will I have time to get there.*

With each thought, images of what might happen if you fail come to the forefront. Each image of failure triggers fear, panic, or even dread. Often, we don't receive the verbal or visual messages, only feelings of the fear and dread. Doesn't take long before overwhelm takes over.

To stop these thoughts, images, and feelings from overloading the mind, avoid tracking your day-to-day tasks and activities in your head. Get them out of your head by writing everything down in the form of an action list.

By getting everything down on paper, the feelings of overwhelm subside. The list lays out the day's priorities so it is easy and clear to see everything. This eases the cognitive load because the mind doesn't feel compelled to track what to do, when it's due, whether there is enough time to do it, or if something has been missed.

Nor does it have to incessantly worry about sending reminders. Once the mind knows that you are aware of the concerns, it no longer has to be concerned about communicating them.

Remember, the erratic thoughts, images, and feelings are the mind's way of communicating to you. Writing everything down acknowledges that communication. It's a big relief for the mind to know that **you know** what's on your plate. That way, it can shift its focus and energy from tracking and worrying to doing.

Often, you'll find that your day is not as hectic and chaotic as it initially seemed. It only felt that way because the mind was tracking everything and feeling overwhelmed that something might get missed. And since the reminders are the unconscious' way of getting your attention, ignoring its attempts simply makes the feeling of fear grow, causing the task to seem more overwhelming than it is.

In addition, writing everything down helps you prioritize the day. It allows you to see what is truly pressing and what can wait. This way, you can direct attention on the difficult or time-consuming tasks. However, when activities are tracked mentally, everything can seem difficult and time consuming.

Action lists also serve as a record of errands that are half finished or left undone. If a report hasn't been printed because it's waiting on approval, the list will indicate that. The same applies to a reading assignment that goes unfinished because you took a break in the middle. A record of loose ends keeps those loose ends from eating away at concentration as the mind doesn't have to track them.

More importantly, action lists keep you from impulsively jumping from one task to another. It's easy to be engrossed in one assignment, but as soon as a reminder for another pops-up, immediately switch to the other. Then when another priority arises, switch to that, skipping from one endeavor to another as they surface.

With action lists, anytime a new priority arises, you simply note it on the list. Once noted, it can be referred to later. This way you can remain engaged in the original pursuit without getting overwhelmed by other issues showing up at inconvenient times.

There are a few ways to tackle the list. One is to focus on the big jobs first, those that demand the most time, energy, and effort. Since they demand more, they tend to incite the most stress. By getting them out of the way, less worry plagues the mind.

Another option is to tackle the small or easy items first. The idea is that small jobs take less time to tackle, so multiple items can be crossed off in a short period. This means fewer items nagging for attention, and hence, leaving more room in awareness for the bigger pursuits.

Yet another option is to change it up. Start with a big or demanding task, then when a break is needed, jump to a smaller, less demanding one. Completing the smaller task will produce feelings of progress and accomplishment to keep motivation high for the bigger projects.

You might instead start with tasks that you dislike or find annoying—the ones you procrastinate and push to later and later times of the day or week. The worst part about procrastination is that although you are not acting, the activity still lingers as a reminder of unfinished business, creating feelings of endless guilt, dread, and displeasure. Getting the task done and out of mind rids you of these draining and distracting feelings.

On the other hand, such tasks can be used to your advantage. Think about it. We avoid tasks we dislike, and since we avoid them so much, we will rather do everything else first. You can use resistance to one task to improve focus on another. Once the others are complete, *will* yourself to complete the first.

These are various approaches to tackling action lists while maintaining strong engagement. Experiment with which works better. You might switch it up based on the day, how you feel that day, and what you have on the burner.

Either way, the key to improving concentration with action lists is to use the list. View it regularly to see which items are open, cross off items that are complete, add new items as they arise, and follow up on those that are half-finished.

The benefits of action lists are short lived if they are never revisited. In the beginning, the mind will feel great knowing everything is on paper. As the minutes and hours pass, however, the natural tendency is to forget those items. As you do, the mind will feel the need to become the planner again.

As a result, awareness and energy will start to be consumed by tracking activities and sending reminders again, and slowly the mind will revert to its old, frenzied state. It will happen sooner than you think, so the list is better served by reviewing it regularly.

Another key is to work with a maximum of 1 or 2 lists. Instead of tracking personal errands, school assignments, and business projects scattered across various sticky notes, journals, notebooks, calendars, smartphones, and in memory, keep them all in one place. A 2008 Virginia Tech study found that recording action items in multiple locations is a recipe for distraction, confusion, and worry.

As a matter of fact, having multiple lists is like having no list. That's because the mind must now keep track of all the lists and the items in each one. Although the mind is not tracking individual tasks, it is tracking the various lists and must remember which items are on which list. This defeats the purpose of action lists, because the end result on your awareness is the same – it becomes clogged and in a frenzy.

Instead of stirring the mind into a frenzy, commit to a single, consistent system for 100 percent of calls, tasks, and meetings, both personal and professional. Choose paper or digital and go the whole hog. Integrate the list directly into a calendar (rather than keeping tasks in a separate list or system). This provides a complete picture of everything on your plate and the ability to prioritize everything in one place. When the mind is confident you are not forgetting or neglecting anything, it is free to focus and engage fully.

CHAPTER 15 - BITE SIZE PIECES

As an author, this is my tenth book, so it's clear I've been writing for many years. Of course, much work is involved in writing and publishing a book. In addition to editing and proofreading the manuscript, an attention-grabbing title needs to be created, an eye-catching cover must be designed, and an enticing book description must be written.

For self-published authors like myself, there is the added responsibility of finding the right editors, proofreaders, cover designers, and copywriters. That means interviewing and hiring candidates and then managing their work.

None of this considers the actual writing, which involves outlining chapters, selecting ideas for the chapters, choosing how to communicate those ideas, whether with facts, data, research, statistics, examples, stories, or analogies, and finally, ensuring everything flows from one to the next.

The final work that goes to the press can seem intuitive, not that big of a deal, or downright obvious. However, I assure you, writing projects don't start off that way. Writing and publishing take enormous time and effort.

Due to the complexity, aspiring authors regularly reach out to me for mentorship. Understanding the intricacies of writing and publishing a book, I am always willing.

What I've noticed is that every author, at one point or another, loses *focus*. The sheer magnitude of the project becomes so overwhelming, they are unable to concentrate. Their awareness becomes consumed by the difficulty, time commitment, and fear of failure than on the project itself.

That said, challenges with concentration often stem from nothing else but the sheer size and complexity of a task or project. It's not that there is something wrong with your concentration or that you are worked up, tracking too many reminders, or lack a clear goal, but the immense scope of what lies ahead. Large projects have the uncanny ability to demolish focus.

That's because large projects do not involve completing just one task, but rather addressing, managing, and implementing a vast number of smaller tasks and pieces. They also involve dealing with many *what-if* scenarios. Similar to getting overwhelmed with too many action items, we get overwhelmed with all the items needed for the project.

Often, we don't even recognize the items, we only feel an overwhelming sense of pressure. At times, we don't even feel that. We just feel distracted without knowing why we are distracted, or even that we are distracted. Other times, we'll simply feel numb, unbeknown to us that, in fact, we are completely overwhelmed.

Sometimes this pressure builds not because of everything that needs to get done, but because we don't know how to get it done. Like deer in headlights, we're unsure of where to start, how to start, or even if it's worth the effort to start. We are well aware that a project is looming, but uncertain about the road to take.

Hence, the mind paces back and forth, like an animal in a cage, contemplating should *I start here or what about there? This is important, and so is that, but I'm better at one, and don't know how to do the other.* With possibilities dispersed in every direction, it's hard to channel energy and effort on any one, which is what concentration requires.

The best solution when the enormity of a task is the cause of poor focus is to divide the project into smaller pieces, and then isolate attention on each piece, one-by-one. It's like creating a grocery list. Do you simply note *pick up groceries*? Of course not. You write everything you want to buy, then at the store, push the cart to each item.

Breaking projects down is similar. Take an overwhelming or intimidating task, assignment, or project, and like a grocery list, break it down into smaller steps. Then complete each step, one at a time, until the project is complete.

As you work on each step, focus only on that step. Don't worry about any other steps like when to do them or if you will have the time or the necessary skills. Worry only about completing what's immediately ahead of you and doing it correctly.

Dividing overwhelming or intimidating projects like this makes them less overwhelming and intimidating. Like writing down your action items, the mind feels assured that you know what needs to get done and when, while also laying out a clear path of how.

More importantly, it's easier to approach a task or assignment when awareness is not clouded with a million other steps and what-ifs. Think about climbing Mount Everest. A glance at the peak will scare anyone silly. If, on the other hand, attention is isolated on getting to just the next base camp, it's easier to do. At the first base camp, the climber is not worried about snow or ice, because he is not that high yet.

Also, each step or milestone acts like a small win. Completing a milestone feels good, and that feeling of accomplishment can inspire you to accomplish the next. This gets the momentum rolling, making the mind and body less resistant to subsequent tasks.

This is exactly what I do when mentoring authors. I give them the next step and nothing else, instructing them not to worry about anything until the immediate priority is handled.

If they are flushing out their outline, they are not to think about the title, cover, blurb, or the sales copy. They can worry about all that only when the manuscript is done, or at least, close to being done. With the first draft, I advise writers not to worry about spelling, grammar, and word choice. Just worry about getting the idea out.

If a step or action item seems intimidating or challenging, it means you haven't broken it down enough. The solution is to divide it further. For instance, a project to host an event might initially be divided as follows: *mail invitations, find venue, hire entertainment,* and *gather speakers.* From there, divide each task further and further and even further, until your step is as easy as *pick up the phone and call 773-555-9301.*

Also, make each step specific and actionable, so when you see it, you know exactly what to do, when, and how. The step *discuss operating agreement* is not as actionable as *call Jennifer at noon to get feedback on the operating agreement.* The step *complete science homework* is not as actionable as *1) Read chapter 7 of the textbook, 2) Review notes from class, and 3) Answer end of chapter questions.*

There are several challenges to be aware of when concentrating on large projects. The biggest is your inner critic asserting that *the task is too big, you are not cut out,* or that *it's a waste of time.* It may also remark *who do you think you are* or *what are you trying to prove,* even going as far as to say, *just let go and have fun.*

The inner critic can sap energy and motivation at every turn. It will criticize your every move. Having criticism filling awareness in of itself is distracting, but having to battle the critic every time you take a step can be downright exhausting. Every step you take, you must jump through a series of hurdles to act. This can slow progress severely and deplete motivation and drive quickly.

Another challenge to tackling a large project is that the mind will get extremely impatient. It can't deal with the pressure of such a big project hanging over its shoulder, so it will want the project done and complete as quickly as possible. This usually happens when there is a lot of stress, anxiety, and pressure to perform, or if the outcome is uncertain or brings heavy consequences.

Like the inner critic, impatience on its own can be extremely distracting, consuming your entire awareness to make it difficult to think, collect your thoughts, or make rational decisions. The only thing running through the mind is how many minutes are left or how many steps remain. With so much anguish, it's no wonder all you can think about is getting to the finish line.

Thinking only about finishing prevents you from enjoying the task or process. In fact, it makes it difficult to enjoy life. You go to lunch and the project is sitting across from you. You are at the movies and the project is sitting next to you. You are in bed with your spouse, and guess what, the project has replaced him or her. No matter what you do or where you go, it is hanging over your shoulders, weighing you down like boulders on your back.

I don't have an easy solution to overcome the challenge of impatience as I still struggle with it myself and haven't found any practical remedy outside of the suggestions already offered. Therefore, I don't want to give you superficial advice that sounds good in theory, but just doesn't work in the real world.

Since I can't offer a quick fix or remedy, all I can say is be aware how the impatience to complete a task can create so much distress and pain that it in of itself becomes a distraction. An overwhelming desire to finish a project can keep you from finishing it.

That's why it helps to break the project into smaller pieces and focus only on the pieces, one at a time. Anytime impatience becomes distracting, think about the pieces.

CHAPTER 16 - VOLUNTARY DETENTION

In my high school, like most high schools, if you missed class or misbehaved, you were sent to what is called detention. The students who really misbehaved were sent to what's called Saturday Morning Detention. That's where they had to show up to school on a Saturday and sit in class for 4 hours.

Nobody liked getting one of those because it meant waking up early on a Saturday, going to school on a Saturday, then sitting in class on a Saturday. If that wasn't bad enough, the sitting was in complete silence.

No talking.

No texting

No tweeting.

Nothing.

Interestingly, I had a friend who gave himself Saturday Morning Detentions. He wasn't a bad kid or got into any kind of trouble, yet he regularly volunteered to sit in detention.

You are probably wondering why anybody would want to do that! Well, why some people do some things is a mystery. With him, it wasn't. There was a rational reason he did it.

He did it because it was the perfect environment to get all his reading, studying, and homework done for the week. Since there was nothing to do, he was forced to pull out his books and assignments he made sure to bring. No matter how miserable the assignment, he had literally no choice but to work.

Now, 4 hours doesn't seem like much, but with nothing to do and nowhere to go, you'd be surprised how much one can accomplish. In fact, my friend told me he'd get a whole week's homework and reading done in that time.

Although he had to wake up early on a Saturday and spend the morning in school, after the detention, he was free. He could relax the rest of the weekend and into the following week with little to no worry on his mind.

Like my friend, a great way to improve focus and concentration is to give yourself voluntary detention—a self-imposed period where there is nothing to do but the task at hand. In this period, you have only two choices:

1. Sit staring stupidly at the wall

Or

2. Defiantly do something productive

Most of the time, we will defiantly do something productive, otherwise each second that passes feels excruciatingly painful.

To create such a scenario, block out a period of the day between 3 to 5 hours where nothing and no one can interrupt you. It helps to leave the house or office and find a place away from friends, family, co-coworkers, or anyone who can be a disturbance. A place where you are forced to be quiet, like a study hall or public library.

Bring to that place only the items you want to work on and leave everything else behind, including your phone. Also bring more work than you think you can finish in the detention period. The reality is what could take 6 hours to complete outside detention might only take 2 or 3 hours in a distraction-free environment.

It helps if you are dropped off at the location so you can't leave until picked up. Then you really have no choice but to focus. Make sure you know exactly what you have to do, though, and bring everything you need.

If you are struggling to focus for long stretches, this might be the perfect solution.

Another benefit of voluntary detention is the depth you can go into a task or activity. Since the mind is not thinking about other things or preparing for possible distractions, the freed up mental energy can take you far deeper into the pursuit than otherwise.

CHAPTER 17 - BREAKTIME

A little over a decade ago, two friends and I were driving back to Chicago from a ski trip in Colorado. While driving through Nebraska, we drove straight into a blizzard so heavy, the highway was shut down, stranding us in a rundown diner in the middle of nowhere for two nights. A few others were forced off the highway and stranded in the diner with us.

It was an interesting group we were. There was a truck driver, a young movie producer and his cinematographer girlfriend, a father with his well-traveled teenage daughter, a business executive with his yogi wife, and a nurse in her mid-twenties.

Since there was nothing to do and nowhere to go, over the few days, we bonded and became friends. The truck driver happened to love magic, so he performed magic tricks and revealed secrets on how they were done. The movie producer clued us into life in Hollywood and his encounters with famous actors. And the teenage daughter enlightened us with stories as a solo traveler to places like Istanbul, Turkey.

As the days progressed, our bond grew stronger and we shared more details of our personal lives. From the trucker, we learned about the trucking industry and the day in the life of a driver. More importantly, we learned about the challenges truck drivers face such as being away from family for weeks to sometimes months on end.

From everything he shared, what I was fascinated by the most was the strict laws that govern the number of hours truck drivers can drive in a given day or week. Even more, strict regulations outline the number and frequency of breaks truckers *must* take. In fact, anyone who drives a truck *must* take breaks between long stretches of driving.

As I later learned, these regulations and limits aren't confined to drivers, but also pilots, medical residents, rail road employees, ship captains, and operators of heavy machinery. Such regulations ensure the safety of workers, their staff, and the public.

These regulations illustrate how crucial breaks are to concentration. Working for hours on end saps energy, drive, motivation, and above all, focus. It becomes increasingly difficult to remain engaged, and as a result, increases the likelihood of missing information, overlooking instructions, or making mistakes. In certain professions, like trucking, those mistakes can be detrimental.

That's not the communication we've received from parents, teachers, and bosses. They've made it seem that we should be able to concentrate nonstop, and if we are not able to maintain uninterrupted focus and attention, we should feel bad, think that there is something wrong with us, or that we are lazy.

The reality is that it's impossible to maintain focus and energy for extended periods. The brain is not built to sustain unbroken attention for hours on end. No book or course can teach that level of concentration.

This is the reason employees in certain professions *must* take breaks.

In many ways, the brain acts like a muscle. When lifting weights or doing yoga, the muscles inevitably get tired. To do each additional lift or hold a posture for each additional second becomes that much more strenuous. However, by taking a break and resting for a few minutes, performing another set of 10 or 20 is easy.

The same principle applies to concentration. Stepping away from a task or activity, even for a few minutes, gives the mind the necessary rest to go another round at full capacity. Otherwise each additional minute requires exponentially more energy, leading you to become more and more tired, losing more and more focus, comprehension, and ability to retain information.

At a certain point, no matter how much effort you exert, you can't go further. Not to mention, pushing for those extra minutes increases the risk of burnout. It's like tearing and straining muscles and putting them out of commission. It's the end of the line for concentration. Though, as mentioned, once a break is taken, even for a few minutes, sharpness and clarity is reset for another round.

That said, when struggles with concentration stem from working hours on end, then the solution is not to apply a technique, but to take a break. No technique that I or anyone else can provide will push focus further. The best technique for the situation is to get up, step away from the task, and give the brain time to recharge.

What's interesting is that breaks not only enhance concentration, but a slew of other mental tasks like creativity, problem solving, abstract thinking, and imagination. As important as concentration is, there are drawbacks to being overly focused as it forces you to operate from one region of the brain or within a limited set of mechanisms and processes. In other words, we get stuck in a one-track mind and can only think about one activity in one way.

Beaks pull the brain out of one-track thinking, allowing it to access other regions, mechanisms, and processes. Having full access to your mental facility is what leads to problem solving, abstract thinking, imagination, and the slew of other mental tasks.

More importantly, breaks are vital for digesting information. Studying, reading, and listening are great for taking information in, but your mind still needs to process and internalize it. By stepping away, the mind gets a chance to process and analyze what is received, and make connections to other information it already knows.

You might not notice the processing happen, as it occurs in the background. However, if you don't give the brain this processing time, it doesn't get a chance to integrate any of the material you learned as its attention is constantly on new information coming its way. Allowing your mind to take breaks, allows you to learn and remember better.

The question is *how long should one step away*? More importantly, *how long should one stay on a task before stepping way*?

There are no straightforward answers as various studies and systems advise on various timing of tasks and breaks. One system, called the Pomodoro Technique, suggests focusing for 25-minute blocks, followed by a 5-

minute break, then repeating this cycle four times, after which you take a longer break of 30 minutes. Another finding recommends working for stretches of 45-50 minutes with 10-15 minutes breaks.

These and other suggestions are sound, but only if you have the self-control to stick to them. Personally, these suggestions are too rigid and require too much discipline for the average person. To stick with cycles of X minutes on with Y minutes off throughout the day, day in and day out, is difficult to follow.

Also, these systems assume that whatever you do or wherever you work, your schedule is flexible enough to divide tasks into these increments. Most of us aren't so lucky. Not to mention, 5–10 minutes breaks are simply too short for some people. It doesn't give their brain enough time to rest and recharge.

A more flexible approach is to break for 10–15 minutes with every hour of work. If you've been on an activity for 2 consecutive hours, take a 20–30 minutes break. With 3 hours, breaktime bumps to 30–45 minutes. It is not recommended to stick to one task or type of activity for more than 3 hours. At that point, take a break even if it's just for 5 to 10 minutes, or just to get up, go to the bathroom, walk around, or stretch.

Another important question is *what should one do during break*? Well, just about anything. As touched on, get up, walk around, stretch the muscles, or go to the bathroom. You might even step out for coffee, grab a snack, do a relaxation exercise, or even meditate for a few minutes. When at home, a bath or shower makes for a nice break. If the time or situation allows, short naps make for nice breaks as well.

What would normally be a distraction any other time is a welcome respite during a break–that includes email, social media, or cat videos. Yep, that's right—even cat videos! The key is to do anything but the task on which you were engrossed. So instead of succumbing to distractions, build them into the breaks.

It also helps to change rooms or environment during a break. Instead of taking a break inside a cubicle, go to the breakroom. If cooped up indoors all day, step outside for a few minutes, even if it's the dead of winter. If you've been out all morning, step inside for a moment. After driving for hours on end, jump out the car, stretch your arms and legs, and walk into the convenience store or gas station.

The best strategy for breaks is to employ the Triune Brain Model and switch between physical, emotional, and logical activities. In the 1960's, Paul Mclean proposed the Triune Brain model, stating that the human brain didn't evolve as one large processing unit, but as a collection of parts.

He proposed that there were 3 distinct phases to the brain's evolution. First there was the brain stem or what is referred to as the reptilian brain. Over that evolved the limbic system or the mammalian brain. On top of that grew the neocortex or the human brain.

The reptilian brain manages all the *physical* functions like heart rate, breathing, and hunger. The mammalian brain is the *emotional* center responsible for emotions. The human brain is where higher-level *logical* tasks take place like language, abstract thinking, and creativity.

Because of these three parts, humans operate in three distinct states–the physical, emotional, and logical. Since we operate within three states, it helps to switch between these states, allowing one part of the brain to rest and recharge, while another is still active and productive.

Physical activities involve walking, running, exercising, dancing, and lifting. They engage or get the body moving in one way or another. Emotional activities involve talking, interacting, playing, listening to music, or watching a movie. Such activities stimulate the emotions. Logical activities include reading, writing, learning, organizing, planning, or problem solving. They use the higher-level mental processes.

To break from a logical activity like reading or studying, switch to an emotional or physical one. That might involve chatting with a friend for a few minutes, watching an entertaining video, playing a game, or standing up, stretching, walking around, or even doing some jumping jacks.

On the other hand, if engrossed in an emotional activity like talking to clients for hours on end, take a break with something mental or physical. Go in your head and read a book, do a crossword, or write an email; you might even spend time organizing, planning, or a bit of rearranging. For something physical, apply the previous suggestions of walking, stretching, even lying down for a few minutes is a physical act.

If, however, you've been immersed in a physical act like moving, lifting, building, or constructing, then what you need is to give the body a momentary reprieve. That can involve any of the previous mental or emotional suggestions, or by simply sitting down and massaging the feet or other muscles.

These examples illustrate the countless options for how and when to take breaks. The bottom line is to step away from the immediate priority and onto something else, something different, or nothing. Doing so gives the brain the needed rest to recharge and process what you've done or learned.

Now, if the nature of the job or time doesn't permit breaks, you can still apply the Triune Brain model to give one part of your brain rest while still being productive. When absorbed in a mental task of writing emails, break with an emotional act of calling a client or attending a meeting. Or, instead of scheduling two meetings back-to-back, which requires emotionally engaging for an extended period, schedule an hour in between to re-energize with a logical task of analyzing company expenses.

As with previous tools, it's important to address the challenges with breaks. Sometimes it's hard to pull yourself away from an activity. You've been working for hours and know its time to break, but the compulsion is to continue working even though focus is rapidly declining and progress is increasingly suffering. It's as if you are stuck and can't pry yourself away. This problem is common among workaholics and perfectionists.

If you are not habituated to taking breaks, then you need to learn the art of stepping away from a task or activity, especially when there is little progress. Sometimes you must snap yourself out and move as far away from the task as possible.

Another challenge with breaks involves having the discipline to return to the task after time is up. It's easy for a 10-minute rest to turn into 20 or 30 minutes, and before you know, hours, days, or even weeks have passed.

You'll see how fun life is when you are not working, and that fun will seduce you to continue extending the break for longer and longer periods. You might even question why you are working so diligently in the first place, and in some cases, reevaluate your entire life.

Don't fall into this trap. Be watchful of your mind talking you into going longer than planned. It will throw up any excuse to extend the break and refrain from returning, especially if it doesn't like the activity or if the activity doesn't fit in line with your beliefs and habits.

It might say, *10 more minutes won't hurt, I'll make it up in the next stretch, I've been so productive, I can reward myself with a longer break,* or *it will only be once.* This is another instance that requires snapping yourself out, but this time, out of the break and back to work.

CHAPTER 18 - FLOW

Athletes rave about a state they enter during competition where everything is on and they can't do anything wrong. They are hitting all the shots, predicting their opponent's moves, and reacting perfectly. Their skill is so well matched to the challenge that the two almost blend together. As Bill Russel, 11-time NBA champion of the Boston Celtics described, *I could almost sense how the next play would develop and where the next shot would be taken.*

Musicians too describe this state, when they play their instrument so well, they become one with it. They hit the notes so effortlessly, it's as if their hands and fingers have disengaged from the conscious and gone off on their own, striking every key with flawless finesse. These musicians become so in tune, they can go off script and sound completely magical. They often report losing all sense of time or awareness in such a state.

This state is not limited to athletes or musicians. Anyone in any profession or activity can experience it, whether a cook, dancer, writer, or actor. Dancers find flow in their flawless performance, businessmen encounter it in their work, during intense negotiations, or the perfect delivery of a proposal. Even students experience it as they inhale information while studying or as answers appear effortlessly during exams.

You've likely experienced this state unknowingly. You reach a level of focus and intention so deep that nothing can divert you. You are not thinking, just doing, and whatever you are doing is to perfection. You may not even notice the time, and if you do, are surprised by how much has passed.

Psychologists call this state *flow*, but many refer to it *as being in the zone*. As described, it's a state where one is in complete harmony with what he or she is doing, making whatever task or activity seem effortless. The person is so immersed and focused that they notice nothing around them. Often, they feel a sense of pleasure, excitement, sometimes even a rush of euphoria or ecstasy.

With such power, much has been studied about this state of heightened awareness. It's been researched for over a century and everyone from world-class athletes to competitive chess players seek to understand flow, and even more, how to elicit this state. Although many can accurately describe what it's like in a flow state, few can truly explain what causes it. Many of the explanations seem only to skim the surface.

I'd like to define flow differently. If you follow the claim made in this book–that humans are a complex set of systems, mechanisms, and processes, most of which occur outside our conscious control–then it begs to reason that flow is the conscious disengaging from a task and allowing the unconscious to take over.

Few realize the power, efficiency, and eloquence of their unconscious. Although one needs the conscious to learn something, once it's learned, the unconscious can take over. That's what a habit is, the unconscious processes taking over a skill.

What's more is that the unconscious doesn't need to think before acting. It can simply act. Doing a task consciously requires deliberately thinking about each step before acting on that step. *Put finger on this key before striking that key* or *place foot here before twirling there*. With the unconscious, no intermediary step to think is necessary. It just performs, allowing a person to act and respond at light speed.

This explains how musicians can rock out without thinking, because they aren't. The unconscious has taken over the thinking. This also explains why people lose awareness or don't remember their time in the flow state. Awareness is no longer with the conscious. It has let go fully, and like a baton in a relay race, passed it to the unconscious.

When people talk about connecting with infinite energy, tapping into higher consciousness, or seeing with the third eye, I believe they are referring to connecting with the unconscious. The unconscious mind is that infinite energy, higher consciousness, and the third eye, and when allowed, can assist us with all its precision, efficiency, and glory.

Not only does the unconscious fully take over in flow, but few to no resistances arise. That means unrelated thoughts, images, and feelings are not competing

129

or battling with the task. Nor are impulses and urges pulling you toward another activity. Even more, the body isn't doing its own thing.

If thoughts surface, they are talking you up, not down. If images appear, it's to communicate options as quickly and accurately as possible. Feelings show up to inspire and support. Impulses drive you to stick with the activity, not run away. Involuntary body movements are precise and calculated and emerge for the sole purpose of making it all work.

So, the state of flow is a combination of the unconscious mechanisms fully taking control off a task, while at the same time, ceasing all self-sabotaging behavior. The necessary skills are readily available, while those that are unnecessary go silent. Everything is fully aligned to support perfect execution and completion.

This is flow. The ultimate in focus, concentration, and attention. It's where records are broken, goals are reached, and dreams realized. With such an introduction, I bet you can't wait to learn how to get into such a state of triumph.

Unfortunately, flow is one elusive animal. There is no specific technique or prescribed guideline to enter flow. It tends to just happen–often randomly and at random times. There are many variables to flow and a delicate balance between those variables.

Although elusive, there are ways to increase the chances of getting into flow. Certain conditions or elements seem to always be present with a person in flow. When those conditions or elements are present, in the right combination and moment, you aid your chances of getting into flow. Let's look at these conditions in more detail.

Mood

First and foremost, flow is mood dependent as a good mood allows a person to enter this state more easily. Think about what happens when you find $20 on the ground or are asked out on a date. Mood brightens and the rest of the day seems to go without a hitch. Suddenly, pouring into a task or project becomes a breeze. Since you are positively immersed, you do better work and get more done. This sense of heightened accomplishment takes you deeper into the state.

Fun

Activities in the state of flow are fun and enjoyable. There are no feelings of dread, animosity, or dislike towards the activity nor towards the person that assigned it. Nor is there a sense that time is being wasted or could be better served on something else. Sensations of pain and struggle are absent. The great thing about flow is that it doesn't necessarily come from enjoyable tasks, it can come from tasks you dislike or even hate, though in the moment, you are not aware of those feelings.

Challenge

When do you usually feel engaged–days before a deadline or the hour before? As the chapter on timeboxing explained, an element of stress and pressure sharpens focus and concentration. It kicks in the defense mechanism, cranking up enthusiasm and drive. Remember, it's the challenge or constraint that elicits the sense of stress or pressure that cranks the enthusiasm and drive.

Relaxed

Although there is a degree of stress in flow, it is not overwhelming. In fact, people in flow tend to be relaxed with research revealing less energy is expended in flow than in other moments. Heart rate slows, blood pressure decreases, and facial muscles relax. The sense of calmness quiets the conscious and eases other mechanisms so they don't interrupt or get in the way of what needs to get done.

Purpose

Flow is driven by a sense of purpose or drive for an outcome. I mentioned that in a state of flow, thoughts, images, feelings, impulses, urges, and involuntary body movements are aligned. I also mentioned this happens naturally when you have a clear goal and purpose. Purpose aligns all the different parts of the mind, which align all the different processes.

It's like a lion on the hunt for its next meal. It is not concerned about how its main looks or what the other lions are doing. All awareness is on the hunt, because if it doesn't catch the next meal, it doesn't make it to the next day. A clear and explicit purpose is what's required to push distractions to the side and channel energy and momentum in a single direction.

Visualization

When world class athletes are asked about the secret to their performance, like Bill Russel, they say that they see it happen in their head before it happens. Communicating intention to the unconscious aid's performance. As explained in the visualization chapter, the best way to communicate to the unconscious is through images. Images give the mind a clear picture of what you want to happen, so it can precisely make it happen.

Pictures not help you communicate with the unconscious, but for the unconscious to communicate with you. For example, if your unconscious wants to communicate the next move you should take, seeing the move and its precise execution translates better than a verbal description of *go here, do that, like this, in such a way*. This allows you to act and react at the speed of thought.

Self-Control

Flow requires a certain degree of self-control and command over the body and its actions and reactions. It requires keen awareness of what you do and how you do it. Although distracting and sabotaging behaviors subside during flow, there are moments when they accidentally show up. An impulse will attempt to pull you in a different direction or a thought suggest that you're going too fast or too hard, and to slow down. Flow requires restraint of such accidental or spontaneous reflexes.

Negativity

Worries, frustrations, and defeat are not characteristics of flow. They are anti-flow. Negativity brings you down, holds you back, and saps energy. It also complicates decisions, stifles action, and narrows awareness and thinking. This doesn't mean that in a flow state a person doesn't worry.

Concerns exist, but they arise to caution and advise, not to overwhelm and defeat.

Belief

Chapter 3 discussed the power of beliefs and how all our decisions and actions get filtered through beliefs. Since your mind is always seeking permission from beliefs to act, it helps to have positive beliefs that regularly give the green light to act and to act without doubt or despair. Believing that you can achieve something, including achieving the state of flow, is an important factor in attaining it.

Random

There is a level of randomness or luck to flow. Let's say in a volleyball competition you accurately predict the opponent to spike the ball. So, you jump to block her attempt. However, she mistakenly loses her step and is unable to go for the spike. Although your prediction was spot on, her mistake changed the outcome.

Had you blocked the spike, the accurate reaction would have provided a rush of confidence and surge of authority, likely resulting in flow. Since the block was not made, you second guess the decision, resulting in frustration, doubt, and hence, a lack of flow.

The opposite can also occur. You make an inaccurate prediction, but through the opponent's own mishap, the sought-after outcome transpires. So, you're ultimately hit with that rush of confidence and authority. Randomness like these can create a challenge to entering flow.

Lack of Strain

One thing is for sure–flow can't be forced. Forcing goes completely against the concept of flow. When you force, you are not flowing. The very nature of flow means not trying, so *trying* to enter flow in of itself prevents it from materializing.

These are the main conditions and elements present during or help trigger flow. As stated, a delicate balance among these conditions and elements is required, which is different for different people, at different times, in different situations, and with different activities. So, there is no guarantee about when and how it will arise.

If you notice, these are all things this book teaches. The chapters on self-talk and visualization transform *beliefs*, with the visualization chapter also training *visual* ability. The goal setting chapter taught *purpose*; *self-control* reverberates throughout the book, but specially in the chapters on impulse control and training the body; the first chapter of this section offers a *relaxation* exercise; and removing unproductive thoughts like *negativity* was discussed in the chapter on awareness.

Although there is no fixed recipe, regularly practicing and applying the exercises and tools suggested in this book widens the door to enter flow. Quelling distractions, ignoring interruptions, and simply giving into the moment unlocks the hidden powers of the unconscious to take your abilities to concentrate deeper and further than you ever imagined.

In addition to regularly applying the suggested exercises and tools, the following can also aid your efforts:

1. Let go and lose yourself in the task.

2. No matter how much you hate a task, find something positive or enjoyable. Was there a time you enjoyed it? If so, think about that time or what you enjoyed about it. If not, think about how much joy you will have once it's finished.

3. Don't look at the clock or think about the time. There is a tendency to lose track of time in flow and constantly inspecting the clock can pull you out.

4. Don't censor or worry about mistakes, just let what needs to come out to come out. Let go of the outcome and your fears about what people are going to say or think.

5. Find a way to make the task challenging. If your talents and skills are not up to the task, you will feel anxious and fearful of failure. If

by some chance your skills far surpass the challenge at hand, you'll become bored and restless.

Think about these five suggestions anytime you begin an assignment.

Selecting the Tools

This finishes the section on *in the moment* tools. Another handful of strategies to crank out concentration, but this time, for moments you need it most.

Let's summarize all the tools in this section.

- **Chapter 11** began with relaxation and provided a simple script to calm your thoughts, images, feelings, impulses, and bodily movements to create a state of heightened focus.

- **Chapter 12** introduced a very novel tool, directed questions, that uses questions to direct your focus.

- **Chapter 13** discussed goals and how reciting a goal can align all the different mechanisms toward a specific task or activity.

- **Chapter 14** talked about the importance of getting all your action items out of your head and on to paper.

- **Chapter 15** instructed to take large goals and break them into smaller parts and to think only about one part at a time.

- **Chapter 16** is about giving yourself voluntary detention, a self-imposed period where there is nothing to do but the task at hand.

- **Chapter 17** is about the opposite, giving yourself breaks, a self-imposed time where you do everything but the task at hand.

- **Chapter 18** addressed flow, the ultimate in focus and attention.

Unlike the suggestion in the last section, you don't have to stick to any one for an extended period. You can cycle through them to see which your mind responds to in a particular moment or with a particular activity.

That means you can apply multiple suggestions in a given day or even on a given task. Use one tool to start an assignment, another in the middle, and yet another to grind it out to the end.

SECTION IV –
DISTRACTIONS

CHAPTER 19 - WHAT ARE DISTRACTIONS?

Distraction refers to anything that diverts attention. Distractions are all around, every hour of the day. They can take the form of a consuming thought, unresolved feeling, interruption like a phone call, or annoyances in the environment like piercing sounds, irritating smells, bright lights, or not enough light.

The idea that concentration is aided by reducing distractions is, on the surface, obvious. After all, a distraction is by definition anything that interferes with concentration. Since it interferes with concentration, it makes sense, then, to reduce or remove as much as possible.

However obvious it seems; this is an area where people still struggle. That is because there is not a lot of good advice on managing distractions. Much of the suggestions skim the surface and simply advise readers to turn off notifications without discussing the deeper causes and triggers of distraction. Like previous sections of this book, this section will not skim the surface, but instead provide a comprehensive discussion on the topic, beginning with why distraction occurs.

Scientists have learned the part of the mind responsible for concentration resides in a different region of the brain than the part that triggers distraction. In a 2007 study, Earl Miller, a neuroscientist at the Massachusetts Institute of Technology, reported that concentration and distraction occur independently of one another and in two separate areas of the brain. In fact, the distraction mechanism is always on, hard-wired into the brain as a process that never sleeps.

What this means is that you have two separate and distinct *mechanisms* battling each other. One mechanism supports and assists concentration. The other pulls it away. Since they can't both have their way, there is an endless tug-of-war between the two. When concentrating, you aren't distracted. If distracted, you are not concentrating.

You are probably wondering *why we have a mechanism that distracts us* or *what could be its purpose?* Well, the distraction mechanism is important for survival. It calls attention to both dangers and opportunities.

Imagine you are planting flowers in the front lawn. You are deeply absorbed in the activity because not only do you enjoy gardening, but want to ensure everything looks nice. Suddenly, your wife pulls up on the driveway, and as she pulls up, loses control of the steering, so now a two-ton steel object is headed straight at you.

It is critical that the mind distract you, no matter how enjoyable or important the activity, to notice the immediate danger. This way, you can react and get out of the way. Miller says, *if something leaps out of the bush at me, that's going to be really important and I have to react to it right away. Your brain is equipped to notice things salient in the environment.* Distraction is a survival mechanism that helps you stay safe.

It also alerts you about potential opportunities. You might be walking down the street thinking intensely about an upcoming presentation only to be distracted by a hundred-dollar bill on the ground. Even though the bill causes you to lose your train of thought, there is now extra spending money in your pocket. Or you might be reading the paper at a café to be distracted by a new book or advertisement for a product you've always wanted but could never afford.

As you can see, the distraction mechanism is useful. It serves as an alert that calls attention to anything that could be dangerous or advantageous. As useful as distractions are, society has put a negative label on this word. Like taking breaks, we are taught to think of distraction as bad, negative, and to look down upon it. More importantly, we are encouraged to hide or turn off this characteristic.

Unfortunately, this mechanism can't be turned off. It is an inherent quality in all of us, so it is not something that can be removed completely. As stated, the distraction mechanism is hard-wired into the brain as a process that never sleeps, even when we're asleep. Since the mechanism cannot be turned off, the best one can do is manage it.

Distractions come in two forms–external and internal. External distractions are those occurring outside of you. They include everything from a piercing noise to an irritating smell to the temperature being uncomfortable. Anything in the immediate surrounding that makes it difficult to pay attention is an external distraction. An unpleasant setting can also be a distraction.

Internal distractions are the opposite. Although they can also be piercing, irritating, and uncomfortable, they originate from inside. You may be feeling hungry, tired, or lacking the motivation to stay with it. Your head hurts or back aches, or worse, have unruly emotions weighing you down. Worse still, you have an insatiable want to call your mom or go on a hike. Or maybe you haven't satisfied a social media fix.

Managing distractions requires managing both types. It is important to not only silence what's occurring outside, but also inside. This section tackles distractions from both perspectives. It explores in profound detail the causes and triggers of external and internal distractions and offers strategies to limit their impact. Distractions are an inevitable part of life and so it's crucial to understand how they interfere with concentration, and more importantly, how to keep them in check.

CHAPTER 20 - REMOVING EXTERNAL DISTRACTIONS

As the last chapter mentioned, distractions come in two forms–external and internal. When it comes to distractions from external causes, there are two ways to manage them. One is to *remove* as much from the immediate environment as possible. The fewer distractions that are around, the less there is to seduce the distraction mechanism.

The other is to *ignore* or to cope with distractions. Remember, the distraction mechanism can't be turned off. It is running nonstop, analyzing everything that may require instant response. More importantly, not every distraction can be removed all the time and in every situation. In these cases, the best option is to work despite their presence. This chapter will look at how to *remove* distractions, and the next chapter will examine how to *ignore* them.

To understand the importance of removing distractions, I'd like to tell you about a niece of mine who loves chocolate. Anytime she sees chocolate, whether it's on the kitchen counter, at the checkout aisle, or even on a television commercial, something flips in her mind where she must have it. She becomes so consumed by the thought, she is unable to finish what she is doing or go back to playing.

However, when chocolate is not around, everything is fine. She can play with her toys, run around with her sisters, and even hold a decent conversation. The idea of chocolate doesn't enter her awareness, and in fact, she doesn't even miss it.

This is most people's experience with distractions. When distractions are not around, we are not thinking about them. As soon as one arises, however, it consumes us. At times, it can be nearly impossible to return to the original activity.

For instance, you are diligently working and the phone notifies you of a new text message. Thoughts then begin churning about *who sent the message, what it says, is it important, maybe it's time sensitive.* Even if you don't check the message, focus is lost because the mind's thoughts are on the message. Conversely, if the notification never went off, you could work without problems.

That's the interesting thing about distractions, once the distraction mechanism is activated, it's difficult to disengage. As the saying goes, *out of sight, out of mind.* That's why it's so important to remove distractions than trying to fight them after they've shown up.

To remove external distractions, it helps to think about them in terms of their effect on us. We are affected by external distractions through the five senses–sound, sight, touch, smell, and taste. A door slamming stirs the sense of sound, a blinking light excites the sense of sight, and a pungent odor irritates the sense of smell.

If you were deaf, you would not be phased by even the loudest bang. If blind, television in the background or intensity of light will have no bearing. With that said, think about everything in your surrounding that elicits the senses, then remove anything that has the potential to be annoying, upsetting, or distracting.

Let's walk through each sense one-by-one. The following suggestions aren't rocket science, however, it still helps to be reminded of them. I find that I overthink problems sometimes when the obvious solution is staring me in the face. Also, at times, it takes reading about an obvious solution before the mind is open to applying it.

Sound

One of the more irritating distractions come from sound. A noisy neighbor robs focus on homework, that all-night party down the hall makes it almost impossible to think, even the ringing of a phone is enough to send you running for the hills. It instantly breaks concentration no matter how engrossed you are.

Beginning with the obvious, remove or turn off anything that has the potential to make sound that you can do without. Turn off noise-making devices, mute cellphones, and shut windows to outside traffic. If the computer beeps every time an app updates, a message is received, or you are mentioned in a Tweet, change the notification settings.

If you have little control over the sound in an environment, change locations. If the dormitory is too noisy, try the library. If the library is closed, find a quiet all-night café or diner. If noise from traffic enters the bedroom, move to the living or dining room.

If changing locations is not possible, earplugs or noise-cancelling headphones help. Another option is to record your entire day on a digital recorder and schedule tasks at times of the day when you are around the least noise.

Sight

Visual distractions can be as disrupting as auditory ones. Once something catches your eye, it's hard to pull them away. Again, it's better to not have temptations in the first place. So, remove visual cues that call attention to anything other than the task you're working on.

Begin with your desktop—both of them. Having the email icon up while working on the monthly budget is asking for trouble. Similarly, leaving crosswords beside the table is begging for problems. Close all programs you aren't using, get unnecessary icons off the screen, and clear your work space of anything that doesn't deal directly with the current task—including other tasks.

Next, get organized. A messy room has the effect of overwhelming the mind. Piles of paper here, stacks of books there, mounds of garbage everywhere pull the mind in a million directions. Unbeknownst to you, they rile frustration, aggravation, and other emotions. Therefore, keep your room as neat as possible. The less clutter in your space, the less clutter in your mind.

Also remove distractions from your line of sight. When thinking about something, in what direction do you look? If your gaze goes to the ceiling, there is probably little in the way of diversions. If, on the other hand, it goes straight for the T.V. across the room or a mesmerizing painting on the wall, potential for distractions exist. Either move the distraction, yourself, or block your view of it. That might involve closing doors, pulling curtains, changing seats, adjusting position, or whatever else to obstruct the view.

Do the same with other distractions in your line of sight. Is there a tear in a chair that pokes your nerves? Tape, vinyl repair kit, reupholstering, or replacing the chair can put an end to that annoyance. Does a flickering lamp make you want to have an epileptic seizure? Change the bulb. Are holes or cracks on the wall testing your patience? Cover them with a picture or painting or rearrange your desk so your back is turned to them.

Touch

You are probably wondering *how much distraction can the sense of touch cause?* Touch has much more influence than you may realize. The firmness of a chair, stiffness of a table, and the softness of your shoes all deal with touch. Even the notebooks you write on and the pen and pencils used to write deal with touch.

Notebooks and pens are common tools that affect touch, but the principle can be applied to any instrument with which you work. As a painter, work with comfortable brushes, or learn to hold brushes in a comfortable way. If work requires being outdoors, wear comfortable shoes and clothing. If gloves are a must, get ones that are snug and make holding onto objects easier.

Another consideration includes the chair. Chairs that are too small, too low, or otherwise too uncomfortable can be distracting. This is important for many whose job requires sitting for extended periods. Although you may not be able to ask a boss or teacher for a more comfortable chair, you can ensure the height is appropriate.

The correct height sets the shins perpendicular to the thighs. Don't set the height so high that your legs are hanging or so low as to squeeze your knees. Proper height also allows you to sit in front of the desk. You might even consider getting a leg rest, maybe even a cushion or back support, and if your chair has arm rests, adjust them appropriately. Such modifications go a long way in creating comfort.

It also helps to change positions occasionally, especially if you have been sitting in the same position for hours on end. That can involve raising the height of the chair or removing the back support or cushion. No need to make a drastic change—just enough to give the body a rest from sitting in one position for extended periods. Once the body is relieved, you can revert to the original position in more comfort.

Touch also deals with the condition of the environment, whether it's too hot or cold, or too dry or humid. Adjust the temperature to a comfortable setting. If in a location where you don't have direct control of the temperature like an office, classroom, or library, wear clothes in layers. When the temperature gets too cold, add a layer or two. If it is too hot, drop a layer.

You might even keep a small fan or space heater nearby to finely tune the temperature of your immediate environment. In dry conditions, consider a humidifier to soften the touch of the air. If too stuffy, open the windows for short spurts to add freshness.

Smell

The biggest disruptions to the senses arise from sound, sight, and touch, as smell is not likely to be a major or regular disturbance to most. On occasion, you may encounter an unpleasant smell, and in such moments, will have to just bear it.

You can, though, be conscious of keeping odors at arm's length. For example, keep garbage away from a work space, or better yet, keep it outside; in other words, throw out the trash often. Don't let perishable food linger either. And, if you work out of a bedroom, contain unpleasant odors from dirty clothes by washing them often or putting them in a hamper.

In addition to clearing a workspace of unpleasant smells, clear it of overly pleasant ones too. If the inviting smell of apple pie is just too much to resist, then the delicious aromas of a bakery, the kitchen, or rooms adjacent to them will not be good options. Don't leave leftovers in close vicinity while on duty. Put them in the fridge, and if a fridge is not an option, a plastic bag that contains the smell.

Taste

Like smell, taste is another sense that is not likely to be a major distraction in life unless you have random things flying into your mouth. In that case, your situation is going to need more help than this book can provide.

The main thing to keep in mind is that unpleasant tastes can linger in the mouth way past the end of a meal. Try to avoid such foods before a big test, exam, appointment, meeting, or interview. Such tastes are not a good way to go about business.

Likewise, consider avoiding pleasant tastes as well. There is nothing more distracting than aftertastes from a delicious meal or snack creating cravings to stop what you are doing to get more. That applies to leaving an open bag of potato chips or packet of M&M's nearby and needing to keep reaching for that bag every few minutes.

Again, taste is not a major area of concern, but if you have a task that requires utmost attention, consider these extra steps. A simple remedy is to drink a glass of water to clear the palate.

This sums up removing external distractions. Thinking about them in terms of the 5 senses–sound, sight, touch, smell, and taste–is an easy way to know what to remove. It is a big step towards laser sharp focus. Now let's turn attention to ignoring distractions.

CHAPTER 21 - IGNORING EXTERNAL DISTRACTIONS

Removing distractions is the best option if you have control over your environment. However, in many situations, there are limits to what you can control. At a cafe, you can't hush all the customers to work out that in the moment brilliant idea. On a plane, it's difficult to throw a crying baby out the window. Also, I'd love to see how effective telling construction workers to stop working because you have to meet a deadline is going to be.

Even if you can prepare the perfect environment, the slightest, most random disruption can make all your efforts obsolete. So instead of learning to *eliminate distractions*, which isn't always possible, this chapter will train you to concentrate despite distractions, which is far more useful.

The following suggestions are like the exercises and tools in the previous two sections, however, instead of developing the ability to focus, these exercises and tools develop the ability to resist distractions.

Be Here Now

Be here now uses a spoken phrase to call a wandering mind back to the job at hand. It is a form of in the moment self-talk that interrupts a distracted thought and guides the mind back to whatever it was doing. It's a deceptively simple technique that works wonders.

Whenever attention wanders, tell yourself, *Be here now*.

That's it!

The door slams. *Be here now*.

A coworker is talking too loudly. *Be here now*.

You're worried about tomorrow's big event. *Be here now.*

This technique works especially well in situations with multiple external distractions. Instead of trying to control, eliminate, or step away from each one, simply command the mind to *be here now*.

Over time, this technique internalizes as a habit. Saying *be here now* and immediately returning to work creates a pattern so anytime the mind hears the signature phrase, it knows to disengage and get back to work.

The Spider Technique

Spiders are fascinating creatures, especially web-building ones. They are always aware of every inch of their web. A touch on one corner vibrates all corners, signaling they have an intruder (or a meal).

You can think of the distraction mechanism like a spider, and the environment, a web. Any change in the environment, be it someone walking by, noise from the next room, or birds outside the window, immediately draws our attention. As you learned, this can be good because no meal (opportunity) or problem (danger) can slip by.

On the other hand, it also means we are constantly put on alert by events that have nothing to do with us or our work. This becomes a real problem when it comes to staying on track.

Spiders are also good at learning to distinguish what's important and what isn't. Striking a tuning fork and holding it next to a spider's web will cause vibrations in the web that will cause the spider to investigate. However, there's nothing for the spider to find. Repeat the process and the spider will investigate once or twice more, but after that, the spider will stop. It learns that the vibration doesn't mean anything, so it ignores it.

Learn to manage distractions like a spider. Ignore the need or urge to investigate every, familiar, or day-to-day sights, sounds, and occurrences. Anytime anyone passes by, instead of allowing the distraction mechanism to look up to see who it is, remind yourself that it is not important. If a flock of birds outside the window get overly rowdy, you can look up, bang on the window, or react in other ways. Or, you can remind yourself, or the mental process that needs to see the commotion, that *it's the same birds that are there every day.*

That's it.

Just like the tuning fork never actually touches the spider's web, these events don't actually intrude on your workspace. Telling yourself they are *out there* and not a part of what you are doing trains you to ignore them. This reduces the effects of distractions and allows you to stay on course. This technique is especially helpful in super noisy and busy environments.

Distraction Training

Some people can be thrown into a crowded stadium filled with screaming fans and still be able to read an entire book from start to finish. You've probably experienced these moments yourself, zoning out and staring into space, then returning to reality realizing you weren't aware of any sight, sound, or movements—not even someone shouting your name.

This can be trained to do on command. In fact, it is possible to do on any activity, whether it be that boring assignment or annoying project. Although, it does require a bit of practice.

To practice, find a busy, high-traffic area that is noisy. It can be a hectic restaurant, a loud coffee shop, or a crowded bus stop, some place with so much visual and auditory noise that you can't hear yourself think or imagine being able to concentrate.

Once there, pick a spot to direct attention for a few minutes. It could be a street sign or billboard, or if inside, a painting or decoration on the wall, or even an object on the ceiling–a spot whose line of sight won't be obstructed by people or vehicles passing by.

After selecting a point of focus, hold attention there without wavering. Keep still, regulate your breathing, and fix your eyes and thoughts on that point. Ignore all other commotion and stay immersed on that spot for as long as possible.

If you notice people talking in the background, tune them out. If a screeching sound of a baby triggers feelings of wanting to strangle it, do the best to tune that out as well. If other thoughts enter your head or if the mind starts to drift, slowly bring it back to the exercise.

Remember, when you lose focus, don't beat yourself up. It happens and is going to happen. Losing focus is not what's important. What is important is to re-center the mind, clear your thoughts, then bring awareness back to the exercise and attempt to hold attention for longer in the next go.

This is a great exercise to condition yourself to focus despite distractions. It's like Exercise 1 in Chapter 5, except instead of ignoring commotion from inner thoughts, images, and feelings, you are ignoring commotion from the outside world. Like the previous exercise, it's not easy—possibly downright frustrating. You'll find you are able to resist distractions for only seconds.

Know that we all start this way.

If you can ignore the frustration and not let it get to you, you'll be able to ignore distractions for longer and longer periods. What you'll find is the frustration in of itself is the distraction. It's not the hectic situation or environment that is disrupting, but your frustration about that situation or environment. It's important to not let the frustration get in the way.

So, the exercise not only trains you to ignore distractions in the environment, but how those distractions affect your emotions. The longer you can hold focus on this task, the longer you'll be able to hold focus on other tasks, especially in those frustrating moments.

That wraps up ignoring external distractions. When distractions arise, sometimes the best solution is simply to ignore them. You learned three tips–Be Here Now, the Spider Technique, and Distraction Training– to help you do just that. Next time distractions rear their ugly head, you will know exactly how to deal with them. Now let's turn the conversation to internal distractions.

CHAPTER 22 – INTERNAL DISTRACTIONS FROM PAIN

As you learned, internal distractions stem from inside, and as such, are much more difficult to manage. Since they come from inside, they are not something you can necessarily remove. More importantly, they are not something you can ignore either, nor do you want to.

Think about the check-engine light of a car, which signals that some process in the engine is not functioning. It's the same for us, when something is not functioning, our unconscious will warn us with a distraction. Since we are so complex, there is a lot for it to warn us about.

In fact, I can write an entire book on internal distractions, and with the first iteration of this book, I did. It was too much content, so I condensed the material into four chapters that address the four biggest internal distractions – pain, emotions, unfulfilled wants, and addictions. The next four chapters discuss each of the distractions, why they exist, and ways to manage them.

This chapter begins the discussion with physical pain and discomfort, which includes everything from a headache to sore muscles, from hunger and upset stomach to being too hot or cold. It also includes feelings of itchiness, inflammation, and stiffness. Though the most common type of physical pain and discomfort arises from tense and achy muscle.

Numerous studies show that pain has adverse effects on both memory and concentration. Though you don't need studies to confirm this, as anyone who has experienced pain knows the outcome is more than an unpleasant sensation.

In fact, the whole purpose of pain is to draw the mind's attention away from whatever we are doing to address whatever problem we are having. Since the purpose of pain is to draw the mind's attention, it's important to prevent pain from arising, and when it has, to alleviate it immediately. The following strategies discuss ways to prevent and alleviate our most common pain points.

Hunger & Thirst

Food and water are two vital needs of the body. Food provides energy and water keeps everything moving. Without these two, we wouldn't be alive. Since they are more important to survival than anything else, the mind evolved to prioritize these two needs over everything else.

That's why when we are hungry or thirsty, it's nearly impossible to think about anything else. The mind shifts into survival mode, putting everything to the side and diverting full attention and focus to refueling. After all, how useful is finishing that report if you are not alive to submit it?

This goes without saying, but make sure to eat and stay hydrated. As obvious as it sounds, most overlook these all-important physical needs. If people ate balanced, nourishing meals and stayed properly hydrated, most of their concentration woes wouldn't be woes.

With that said, if you are required to concentrate for extended periods, whether for an exam or that long afternoon meeting, bring along snacks and a bottle of water. It's also a good idea to avoid foods that dehydrate the body, like coffee or alcohol.

At the same time, don't overdo it. Eating too much, too quickly causes blood to rush away from the brain to digest food in the stomach. This leads to *food coma*, which hampers performance. In the same light, drinking too much increases the need for bathroom breaks. This is one of those areas where a delicate balance of enough, but not too much is required.

Stretching

The easiest way to prevent and alleviate most physical pain is with some quick stretches. In my opinion, lack of stretching may be the biggest contributor to physical pain. That's because the body is built to stretch regularly. When it does not, muscles become sore, tense, and inflamed. This reduces circulation, blood flow, and oxygen to the cells, affecting proper functioning of the organs and other parts of the body.

Stretching is so vital that all animals instinctively know how to stretch and frequently stretch throughout the day. Before birds take flight, they spend a few minutes stretching their wings. When cats wake up, they go through a routine of extending and elongating their head, neck, legs, and back. In addition to stretching, dogs shake to loosen their muscles. In fact, most postures in yoga are named after animals like *downward dog, cobra, cat, cow, camel, and frog.*

Though, for some reason, humans have stopped stretching or lost sight of its importance. Many don't even stretch when waking in the morning, which is an instinctual response and the most important time to stretch. Regardless of the reasons, get into a daily rhythm of stretching, not just for concentration, but overall health.

Stretching the lower back is the best place to start as it is the bridge between the upper and lower body. So, stand up and bend forward at the hips. Just dangle there and allow the force of gravity to pull you down to give the back and legs a nice stretch.

Another easy stretch involves crossing the fingers, raising the hands in the air, and reaching towards the ceiling. Continue reaching for the ceiling as you feel a stretch along the hands, wrists, and forearms, then down the biceps, triceps, neck, shoulders, chest, abdomen, and back.

If you are standing, keep pulling up until you feel a stretch in the hips, front of the legs, back of the legs, and the knees. Then, raise the heels off the ground to stretch the calves, ankles, and feet. If lack of flexibility keeps you from raising arms up to the ceiling, lift them as far up as you can and start the stretch from there.

These are two simple stretches anyone, no matter how out of shape, can do any time. Whenever the body or muscles are feeling sore, tense, or achy, stand-up and either bend forward or reach the hands high.

These stretches are great to do between breaks, tasks, or every hour or so throughout the day. Regular and repeated practice will increase flexibility, decrease pain in the muscles and tissues, and improve circulation to the brain, and hence, concentration.

Posture

Often achy muscles and physical discomfort result from poor posture, such as slouching, hunching, stooping, and drooping. If poor posture is the source of your physical pain, the remedy is to sit or stand straight with the head up, chest out, and shoulders down and rolled back.

The following two shifts easily put a person in optimal alignment.

1. When sitting, think about pushing the butt back. Notice how that one movement naturally elevates the torso and puts the lower back, hips, and abdomen in correct alignment.

2. For the upper half of the body, imagine there is a string attached to the middle of your chest that someone is pulling up. Notice how this naturally brings the chest up and out, and the shoulders down and back. These two simple, deliberate shifts put the body in better alignment.

If you've had poor posture for a long time, you may not be able to hold these positions for too long. Within a few seconds or minutes, the body will want to revert to its old form. It will take time and consistent effort to strengthen the muscles and develop the habits to maintain this posture.

Don't get upset or discouraged if you fall out. Simply push your butt back and lift the chest again. The trick is to immediately readjust the second you notice that you've fallen out. Over time, those muscles will strengthen and habits will build, so the posture will become the natural way you sit and stand.

Headache

Physical pain in the head poses the most challenge for concentration since that's where the brain resides. As a result, physical pain due to headaches tend to cause more disruption than physical pain in other parts of the body.

One remedy is to open the mouth wide and just let the jaw hang for thirty seconds to a minute. This provides a nice stretch from the jawline and side of the face all the way up the checks, temple, and head, relieving pain, tension, and discomfort in different parts of the face and head, especially in areas you didn't know pain existed. This exercise is also great for those who clench or grind their teeth because it releases wound up muscles responsible for the clenching and grinding.

Another option is to give yourself a head massage. First, locate where the pain resides. Is it in the forehead, temples, near the sinuses, or is it in the side of the head? Then massage that area, applying varying degrees of pressure.

If you have a lot of physical discomfort from achy, tense, tight, or wound up muscles, I recommend getting a massage from a trained massage practitioner. A skilled practitioner can release those tight knots and bunches. It's a great way to relax, unwind, and more importantly, take a break, all contributing to better concentration.

If your physical pain is chronic, meaning it's not simply from sitting in an awkward position for extended periods, and you've just accepted it as a part of you, these exercises may not provide immediate relief. They may if you apply them daily for at least a few weeks, though you have to apply them daily for at least a few weeks to know. Don't assume they won't only after a few tries.

Yoga

If these suggestions don't provide immediate relief or with more serious or chronic pain, I recommend a regular practice of yoga which can release deep rooted discomfort, both physical and mental. Yoga has been a great respite from many of my own physical aches and pains.

If you are new to any form of physical activity, start with a non-strenuous yoga practice like Yin Yoga. Then as you gain strength and comfort, experiment with other practices like Hatha, Vinyasa, or Ashtanga. Like any long-term solution, yoga requires consistent practice for at least a few months to see results.

This is all for boosting concentration by relieving physical pain. Pain is one of those things you don't think about until it's there. Once there, it becomes impossible to focus on anything else. These suggestions ensure you're actively taking care of yourself so they creep up on you.

Chapter 23 – INTERNAL DISTRACTIONS FROM EMOTIONS

Another powerful internal distraction comes via emotions. This book has discussed quite a bit about feelings and how they affect awareness. And if you remember, emotions (along with sensations) make up our feelings. This chapter highlights this noteworthy aspect of feelings called *emotions*.

Humans are in a constant flux of emotions. When waking up in the morning, we feel cranky. With a deadline, we feel rushed. When giving a presentation, we feel stressed. When things don't go our way, we feel angry or disappointed. These are few of the thousand triggers we have to emotions.

Given the number of emotions we have and how often we experience them, they can be a serious disruption in life. In fact, I believe emotions are the biggest internal distraction that exists. As discussed in the introduction, when an emotion arises, it takes up room in awareness, leaving less room for other tasks and activities.

Without healthy awareness and proper ways to deal with emotions, they can wreak havoc not just with concentration, but our entire life. I personally believe that insanity is nothing more than a person losing control of their emotions. When emotions come up intensely, violently, or irrationally, they cloud the rationale part of the mind and have us acting erratic, irrational, and even **insane**. That's when people exclaim, *have you lost your mind?* It's not that our mind is lost, only control of our emotions.

What's worse is to suppress emotions. Suppression, as we've learned, doesn't make things go away. Like adding fuel to a burning flame, it only makes them stronger. The more we suppress, the stronger the emotions get. The stronger the emotions get, the more disruptive they become.

What's truly insane is that we don't often choose to suppress many of our emotions. The defense mechanism does it for us. An uncomfortable feeling will arise and the defense mechanism will immediately block it. The defense mechanism is designed to block painful experiences so we can deal with what's important in the moment. It can suppress an emotion without us knowing.

Overtime, suppressed emotions can become an unconscious drain. One part of the mind is trying to express the emotion while another part is keeping it from surfacing. This back and forth consumes tremendous energy—energy that could be used on something more important than this draining back and forth. We may not notice the drain, or even the back and forth, but it is there, stirring underneath.

This can lead to all sorts of mental, emotional, and physical issues such as fatigue, depression, insomnia, reactivity, mood swings, addictions, weakened immune, and chronic pain. All of these add to the challenge of concentrating.

If you are human, you likely have many suppressed emotions right now. And they are affecting concentration and your ability to manage the struggles of daily life. It's not a stretch to say that your life is likely a struggle because of suppressed emotions. It is crucial to find healthy ways to cope with them.

Extremely crucial!

If emotions aren't affecting your concentration now, they will in the future.

In this section, you'll learn to develop a better relationship with emotions.

Identify

The first step is to identify the emotions fueling distraction. Often people dealing with emotions are overwhelmed by a confusing mix of feelings. They may be aware that they are worried about cash flow, but not recognize the bigger feeling of resentment that someone else isn't taking steps to correct the problem. A person going through relationship problems may recognize the anger with their partner, but not see the underlying fear for the future.

A great way to identify your emotions is with exercise 3 in Chapter 5 on observing your thoughts. It's a great way to go inward and see exactly what's percolating in your mind.

Another way to identify all the emotions you are feeling is to write about them. That begins with making a list of everything distracting you. Is your company starting another round of layoffs, landlord threatening to raise the rent, or car acting up again? Or is your son having trouble in school? Whatever it is, write it down.

Next to each concern, note what you are feeling. Write *I feel...* then finish the sentence with how the situation makes you feel. Don't worry about grammar, punctuation, or being neat. Just write. Keep writing until you run out of things to say.

If you don't like writing, try speaking into a voice recorder or talking with a friend. The main thing is to continue putting words to the feelings until you have nothing left to say. As you do, you'll uncover emotions towards people, situations, and incidents you never knew existed.

They've been inside, locked up, with no way of getting out. It's these locked up, hidden emotions that create the *unconscious drain* referred to earlier. They consume energy, resources, mental processing power, and more importantly, personal freedom.

This exercise brings awareness to such feelings, making them easier to deal with. Often, simply allowing feelings to make themselves known is enough to release yourself from their taxing effect. Though most times, they require an additional step, which entails expressing the emotion.

Express

Technically speaking, emotions are meant to be expressed. That's how they are designed. Not to be ignored, not to be bottled, and not to be hidden or censored. So, it's vital to find healthy forms of expression. Emotions can be expressed in one of the following ways:

Verbally

This includes talking, singing, or even screaming if done the right way. If sad, sing a song that expresses the sadness. If angry, scream at the top of your lungs or jam to the tune of heavy music. If frustrated, talk to someone who will listen. Sometimes a prayer can act as a form of verbal expression.

The best form of verbal expression, however, is to talk to the person who triggered the feeling. If someone has upset or hurt you, let them know. Although not always the easiest, it's the most powerful way to release long standing pain and trauma you may be carrying. You don't have to shout at them in anger, calmly telling them how you feel can work wonders. If you can't do it in person, write them a letter, an email, or do it over the phone.

Physically

Many find they can wear out emotions by channeling them into physical activity. They take the adrenaline that comes from anger or fear, and use it to push themselves into action such as running, cleaning, gardening, or exercising. These people find that intense emotions fuel their physical activity, and they can stay in the activity until the fuel, and hence, intensity runs out, leaving them calm and focused afterwards.

Logically

A few can use logic to release emotions. They sit down and examine whether an emotion is helping or hurting them, and if it is hurting them, use that knowledge to release it. This approach takes a great degree of inner awareness and should not be used if it is difficult to make work. It is far too easy to use logic to suppress an emotion and assume it is released, then to actually release it.

Letting Go

Some possess the ability to just make a conscious decision to let go of emotions. They may picture themselves popping a balloon filled with their anger or physically relaxing tight muscles and clenched jaws, pushing the tension caused by emotions out of their body. Or they may simply decide that they are done being afraid and act despite the fear.

Take time to experiment and find the best method or methods to express emotions. You will know you've found a method for a particular emotion, when after putting the method to use, you feel lighter, there is a sense of relief, and release of pressure.

It is worth noting, the process of identifying, expressing, or otherwise coping with emotions can be slow and lengthy. Sometimes, you may find yourself revisiting the same feelings and triggers again and again, releasing only small amounts at a time. Depending on the severity and your sensitivity to the incident, it may take weeks, months, or even years to fully release an emotion.

Don't be discouraged by the time frame as sometimes this is the process of healing from an emotion. With every bit released, however, you will be able to concentrate more, sleep better, and even find enjoyment in life. What you'll discover is that most of your long-standing issues in life weren't to the people, situations, or incidents, but merely the emotional response to those people, situations, or incidents.

More importantly, you'll discover that all your emotions ever wanted was to be heard. They weren't looking for you to act, change, or to go out and do something drastic; they just yearned to be heard. When you take time to listen, they release on their own.

CHAPTER 24 – INTERNAL DISTRACTIONS FROM UNFULFILLED WANTS

One of the most disruptive internal distractions is from unfulfilled wants. As the name suggests, unfulfilled wants are needs and desires that go ***unfulfilled***. They can be for anything and arise for any reason. For example, you might storm off to work because of a fight with a family member, then while at the office, be unable to focus because you have a desire to apologize. There is a want there, and until it is realized, it tugs at you.

This is one teeny tiny, miniscule, oh so small example of all the many types and varieties of wants you have. Truth be told, at any given moment, you're cycling through a horde of wants. You may have a want to watch T.V., listen to a song, hang out with friends, phone home, talk to a significant other, buy new shoes, read a book, get a daily dose of the news, hit the gym, grab coffee, or check the mail.

This list likely only represents the wants you have for today. You also have wants that represent what you hope to have or do during the week or over the weekend. That can include getting together with friends, attending a play, seeing a show, mowing the lawn, cleaning the house, and shopping for groceries.

Then there are longer-term wants you seek to realize over the next month, year, and beyond. That may entail buying a car, finding a long-term mate, getting into a good school, growing into a management position, or paying off debts.

In addition to immediate or future wants, you are holding onto numerous wants from the past. Do you remember wanting a remote-control car or doll house as a child, but never got one? Well, that want is still there, buried deep inside.

Is there a relationship from the distant past that you keep thinking about? Probably, you yearn for closure. Perhaps you didn't realize a goal or meet the expectations of someone you admire. To this day, it's still lingering. As humans, we carry a ton of unfilled needs, wants, and desires from the past with which we've completely lost touch.

Although we've lost touch, they still affect and influence us today. For example, if you felt left out as a child, some mechanism inside is orchestrating your day-to-day behavior, right here and now, so that doesn't happen again. That mechanism will direct your attention and awareness to avoiding being left out over everything else you could be doing.

The same applies to struggles with a close family member, friend, or companion to whom you haven't talked in years. Although you may not have thought about that person in years, an unconscious drain is likely occurring, affecting many parts of your life including mood, energy, health, and even, concentration.

It's not hard to see, we have tremendous amounts of wants, needs, drives, and desires simmering inside. In fact, they go beyond the specific examples mentioned here and include the more general drives listed in Chapter 1 of security, approval, sex, admiration, wealth, fame, and beauty.

Not to mention, the biggest want of a human–romance or life partner. Without the ability to share experiences and life's ups and downs, life can feel empty, and thus, leave a person feeling lonely. This want is usually on the forefront of people's awareness over everything else.

The problem is that unresolved wants, whether from the past or for the present and future, are distracting. They are a much bigger distraction than you can imagine, constantly gnawing, biting, and chewing their way into awareness in hopes of being fulfilled.

Sometimes they are like a dark cloud constantly looming over you. No matter what you do, where you go, what you've done, or where you've gone, the cloud hangs overhead as a never-ending reminder of the unfulfilled desire.

Moreover, with so many wants, it's difficult to pick any single one. As soon as you start on one, the mind begins nagging you about another. When you begin the other, it nags about something different still. You get tugged in every direction–north, south, east, west–yet always standing still, never moving anywhere. The only thing that moves is that of your energy and concentration draining.

To truly focus and remain present, it makes sense then to *fulfill* and *resolve* those unfulfilled and unresolved wants. Or at the very least, tone down their influence and intensity as not to occupy so much space in awareness every moment of the day, stimulating urges and drives that push you in every direction but the direction that matters most.

Though this is not an easy thing to do. Our wants, and the mechanisms responsible for those wants, are complex. In turn, there are complex reasons why we have the wants we do, why we have so many, and more importantly, why they seem relentless. If you think about it, the entire field of psychology has spent centuries trying to understand our wants and drives, and we've only begun to scratch the surface at understanding them.

Due to their complex nature, it is obviously out of the scope of this book to help you realize every distracting want. Nonetheless, this chapter will attempt to help you better deal with and manage them.

Acknowledge Your Wants

The first step is to acknowledge your wants. Similar to thoughts, emotions, and bodily sensations, wants strive to communicate. Just as with thoughts and feelings, too often we ignore or suppress the communication.

Consequently, the want grows and grows, getting stronger and stronger, demanding more and more attention. Even the rowdiest, greediest, and most ravenous yearnings seek only to be acknowledged—not necessarily realized, but merely acknowledged.

It helps, then, to acknowledge them.

The way to do that is to write out everything that you have ever wanted, wished, or yearned. Take out a sheet of paper and note every yearning or need that you have, starting with the ones you have right now. Do you desire to finish a report, order a pizza, call a friend, or devour a piece of chocolate? Write it down.

Then move onto the bigger wants, beginning with the more obvious, traditional ones like the pursuit for a nice car, big home, financial security, fame, admiration, respect, status, and popularity. Think about everything you have ever wanted to have or do in life, but either didn't do, didn't get, or put off for another time.

Even note desires you are afraid to admit to yourself or others. *In particular,* write down the things you are afraid or embarrassed to admit. Since you've shut them out for so long, those are the ones that seek to be noticed the most.

Think also about the wants from childhood. Was there a toy all the kids had that you didn't? Were there moments you felt left out? Did you have a general sense that you were left out of all the fun and excitement? Bring them to the forefront so you can acknowledge and pay attention to them.

As briefly stated, one of the strongest human desires is connection–to be with someone, to have someone in life, to be needed, or to grow with a life partner. Are you lonely? Do you seek a partner? This one is difficult for many to admit. Don't be afraid or shy as most of us have this want, even though we pretend not to. I can't force or pressure you to acknowledge it, but I can say that it's pain won't go away until you do.

If your list isn't at least two pages, then you are not being honest with yourself. Don't rationalize why you shouldn't have the want as you'll do that later. Also, don't focus on just what one part of *you* wants, but what *all* parts of you want.

Remember, inside you there are many you's. Each you has a unique set of drives, aspirations, and wants. Consciously, you may not be aware of a desire, but underneath, yearning for it deeply. No matter from which *you* the desire or yearning stems, put it on the list.

Writing everything down should make you feel lighter, less tense, and more relieved. As mentioned, many of your wants seek only to be made aware, not necessarily realized. Like removing the cover off a boiling pot, bringing wants to the forefront of your awareness releases tremendous pressure—pressure distracting you from other pursuits.

I really want to highlight the value of this exercise, as I have with a few other techniques in this book like self-talk, impulse control, and breaktime. Of all the exercises in this section on distraction, this one is the most important to do. I can't emphasize it enough because it can really help surface long standing baggage that you don't even know exists. Looking at them is the key to letting them go. Less baggage equates to better concentration.

So, take time out right now. Put the book down and pull out a sheet of paper and start writing. In fact, I'm going to do it with you. That is, I've stopped writing just now to do this exercise. That's how important I believe it is.

Although this exercise provides incredible relief, it may not make all your wants go away. It will take the cover off the cooker, but not necessarily reduce the flame. Pressure is down but wants are still bubbling. For that, the next step is in order.

Examine Your Wants

Now that you have listed your unfulfilled desires, it's time to dissect them. With each want on the list, ask why you have that want or where it came from. Is it as important as the wanting mechanism makes it seem? The wanting mechanism has the astounding ability to make the most trivial matter seem extraordinarily vital. Can you live without it? In order words, if that want never transpires, would it be the end of the world?

More importantly, if you could realize this want, would it fulfill you like you imagine. Or is the mind simply manufacturing such an image? The wanting mechanism also has the astounding ability to make the outcome seem much better than the reality. Are the lives of the people who have what you want as great as you imagine? If so, are you certain it will be the same for you? Can you think of times when you got what others had, but didn't fulfill you like it did for them?

Do this with every want on the list. This will help you look at your desires from an objective perspective, instead of an unconscious impulsive one that is randomly driving you to *see this*, *buy that*, *go here*, and *escape from there*. You and your mind will start to realize that many of your wants are irrational and not worth being hung up about. This way you can realistically decide whether a want will be helpful or useful to pursue or have in life.

By deciding that it's not worth the effort, the mechanism will let it go. When it's been let go, it will no longer pull and tug at you, nor make you sad or depressed that you don't or can't have it. This reduces the intensity of the flame.

Can't Have Your Cake and Eat It Too

Let's reduce the flame even further. For the items still poking at you, realize that many of our wants are quite irrational. That is, it's impossible for any one person to have everything you crave as most of those wants and desires are conflicting.

In other words, to have one thing requires giving up another. To have a lot of friends means giving up alone time. To have fame means giving up privacy. To have a prestigious job means giving up free time to maintain it—free time that you could be spending with friends, family, or with yourself. To own a thing requires time and effort to take care of it.

Nonetheless, the mind still creates wants for them. The wanting mechanism doesn't quite understand that our time, energy, resources, and above all, concentration are limited. Yet, it continues churning out wants and desires, one after another, day-after-day, at a pace faster than any one person can possibly realize. When they are not realized, we are left feeling empty, sad, and depressed, which sap even more energy, motivation, and focus.

To add fuel to the flame, we live in a society where the mere act of stepping out the front door opens us to a tidal wave of temptations. We might see a neighbor with a new car, a friend return from a relaxing vacation, a stranger with an attractive girlfriend, a co-worker receive a promotion, or a classmate dressed in the latest fashion. With each encounter, a new yearning, longing, or want pops up and steals focus. For some, these wants can overpower one's awareness with emotions of intense jealousy, anger, and even hostility.

What's worse is that you don't even have to step out the front door. Wants come to you in the way of advertisements, which are everywhere these days—on television, billboards, flyers, websites, and even in songs, movies, and shows in the way of product placement. These advertisements are becoming so cunning and crafty at creating wants and desires, they bypass the conscious mind and plant desires directly into our unconscious.

Some advertisements go beyond even that. They create the sense that you chose to want a product or service, but it was the craftiness of the campaign that influenced the decision. You think the contents of this book are new or novel? Marketers have known about this for decades, and have been using it to grab your attention and pull it in directions you can't imagine. That's why we've become such a distracted society.

The point is, even if you lived 10 lives, you couldn't scratch the surface of your many wants and desires. Your neighbor with the nice car probably isn't the most attractive person in the world. And that friend who came back from the nice vacation, if he or she spent money on a vacation, likely doesn't have money to buy other things. As for that stranger with the attractive girl or boy friend, remember that no relationship is perfect.

Even worse, the wanting mechanism generates cravings for things our systems are not capable of achieving. A person might have a want to be fit, but his habits won't allow it. Someone else might have a want to date, but her beliefs will get in the way. Even though our system is not capable of achieving a want, the mechanism still produces it. This is the grimmest aspect of our wants, as they make us long for things that we can't physically achieve or won't ultimately find fulfilling.

This should keep your concentration, and sanity, in check. That is, hopefully some part of your mind can understand that all the wants another part of your mind is generating aren't serving you. Many of them are conflicting, come from an unrestrained mechanism, are intensified by society and advertisement, and worse, difficult or nearly impossible to achieve or be fulfilled by.

If the inner mechanism can't understand that enough to keep itself in check, hopefully *you* can understand it enough to keep *it* in check and not get hung up, and thus, ruin otherwise perfectly good concentration.

Having More Leaves You More Hungry

If that wasn't enough to shift your mindset, it helps to know that having more doesn't necessarily satisfy hunger. It may for a moment, but like curiosity, it only makes you more hungry. Even if you could do or have everything on that list, your mind would simply come up with more wants to chase. *Having more only makes you want more.*

As of the completion of this book, I've traveled to nearly 100 countries around the world. After traveling to enough places, I inevitably began to see a pattern in history. A standard story that plays out over and over, time and time again, no matter what part of the world I visited. It's the story of sultans, kings, and emperors fighting wars, battles, and conflicts to gain empires, kingdoms, and nations.

As I learned about these rulers and visited their castles, palaces, and mansions, I saw firsthand how lavishly they lived. You can't imagine just how much one person could own in life. Wardrobes to clothe a town, rooms the size of houses, driveways extending for blocks, lawns as extravagant as parks, along with personal maids, cooks, assistants, doctors, therapists to populate a town—the whole nine yards.

As I delved deeper into the lives of these rulers, I started to see something else. I saw just how unfulfilled and miserable these people were. No matter how much wealth, power, admiration, and status they acquired, they were never satisfied. Whether a sultan of the Middle East, king in Europe, or emperor of Asia, the story was the same. They always wanted more, and more, and more. They kept expanding their empire, growing their wealth, and widening their influence. And for what? To have more of what they already had.

For many of these rulers, the need for more led to their ultimate demise. The likes of Alexander the Great, Julius Caesar, and Napoleon Bonaparte conquered some of the largest empires the world has known, yet lost everything they had, including their lives, in the attempt for more.

This behavior can be observed in modern day celebrities, many of whom have the wealth, influence, and social status of kings. Some celebrities make more on a 30 second commercial than most of us will make in multiple life times. Still, they get caught in depression, anger, addiction, premature death, and even suicide. It is safe to say these people sought wealth and success for happiness and fulfillment, yet it wasn't enough.

Having more is not the be all and end all to resolving unfulfilled wants and desires. To reiterate, even if you had everything you wrote on that list, you wouldn't magically become fulfilled. It seems like you would and the wanting mechanism does an amazing job of giving that impression, but the reality is, that the mind would just come up with something else to chase, then something after that, and after that, and after that.

I have personally experienced this raging wanting mechanism. Although I come from a third world country and grew up poor, most anything I have ever wanted in life, I was able to work hard enough to achieve, even traveling to 100 countries around the world, an experience that allowed me to enjoy people, cultures, cuisines, and a life very few can imagine. In many ways, I lived better than kings, trekking to the farthest reaches of the globe to see wonders that most couldn't imagine.

Though no matter how many countries I visited, experiences I had, people I met, or cuisines I tried, it was never enough. After reaching 30 countries, my sights were on 50. Once I reached that milestone, my wants were quenched for mere hours before it set sights on more places. Even as I approached the 100-country mark, my hunger continued, making all I had already seen and done just an afterthought.

I not only continue to have wants for travel, but everything else. I have wants to write another book, even though this is my 10th. What's worse, I have wants to start books when I'm already in the middle of writing one. While working on one book, the wanting mechanism throws out ideas for 5 other projects it compels me to pursue.

It's not just books I'm pulled towards. Although I am vegan, I have wants for a big juicy steak. Despite the fact I don't watch T.V., I am lured into the latest episode on Netflix. Even when I have a girlfriend, seeing other women makes me want to be with them. The appeal is so enticing, I'm led to believe the new girl can offer something I'm missing in my current, and if I don't jump on the opportunity, it will be gone forever.

Now that I understand that our wants are unforgiving, that attaining them is not going to make the mechanism stop, or worse, simply make it want more, I am not as susceptible to them. Like thoughts, I realize that wants come and go. A want to go online will come, and then it will pass. A want to pig out on pizza arises, and then it fades. As a result, they don't distract or pull me away as much.

It does take a degree of self-awareness and impulse control to get to this level, but it is possible. The point is, like impulses, a want can create the feeling that the world will end if it is not realized. Whether or not it is realized, another will take its place. Understanding this is the golden road to resisting an intense, all-consuming want.

Our wants never end. I've come to understand in a way that makes sense to me that they were never meant to, which is outside the scope of this book. However, for the purposes of this book, it's important to not lose control of your wanting mechanism, as it can create mayhem, especially around concentration.

Given all that, I am not saying you shouldn't strive for these things. It's good to have goals, dreams, and aspirations, especially those that challenge and push you forward. In fact, that's the reason you are reading this book, to improve focus, attention, and concentration to do, achieve, and have more in life. And that's the reason I wrote this book, to support you in this purpose.

However, too many and uncontrolled wants can spin you in the opposite direction. Wants can become a distraction to getting your wants. They prevent you from realizing any want, let alone all of them. Don't let unfulfilled wants become a hurdle or challenge in life. *Happiness isn't about having what you want, or even wanting what you have, but having no wants at all.*

That wraps up the discussion on wants. Do you *want* to learn about another deceptively devious internal distraction? Continue to the next chapter.

CHAPTER 25 – INTERNAL DISTRACTION FROM ADDICTIONS

Addiction is the inability to stop engaging in a behavior or using a substance, even though it may be causing psychological and physical harm. Chapter 9 on Impulse Control touched on addictions briefly, though due to their overwhelming nature, the discussion of addiction deserves an entire chapter.

That's because addictions have an enormous impact on concentration and I don't use the word *enormous* lightly. Anytime the need for a fix arises, all the different parts of the mind, mechanisms, awareness, thoughts, images, and feelings fixate on that craving.

When the craving is not realized, it becomes increasingly difficult to think, make decisions, or process new information. If the addiction is strong enough, muscles tense, thoughts race, and pain erupts, causing one to become increasingly irritable, stressed, and even, disoriented.

If you notice from the description, mechanisms responsible for focus are hindered and mechanisms riled by distractions are aroused. In this state, the mind is annoyed and disorganized.

One might assume this description refers to addictions to hard substances like drugs or alcohol. These are some of the more commonly known and dangerous addictions, but as you will learn in this chapter, we can be addicted to anything and it affect our lives just as much as drugs or alcohol.

Anything you *need* to have or do is a manifestation of addiction. If you watch a lot of television, then you can become addicted to it. When you are away, you become agitated, aroused, and jumpy–all states that affect concentration. In addition to television, you can become addicted to sports, internet articles, gossip, bad mouthing people, the news, and food.

In fact, much of the products and services we regularly use are intentionally designed to be addictive. The best examples are video games, many of which are created with the specific intention to keep a person compulsively playing. I say *compulsively* because even if the game stops becoming fun, the person can't stop. He or she continues playing as if in a hypnotic trance.

Acquiring an item in the digital world triggers the same dopamine and emotional rush as acquiring one in real life. Game developers use this fact to get players to chase digital items and goals, such as new ranks or levels, as if it were the real thing. This is why people compulsively spend hours on end trying to earn virtual objects that don't exist.

Even though they don't exist, gamers are conditioned to do it using theories based around Harvard psychologist BK Skinners. He discovered from experiments with mice that behaviors can be shaped and molded with a simple sequence of incentives and rewards.

The trick is to start with little rewards, bit by bit. Once the brain becomes hooked on the emotional rush of the reward, levels or missions are spaced so rewards are farther apart. This compels the participant to play longer to get the emotional hit.

As with gambling, add an element of randomness to the rewards, now the person is hooked. He or she can't stop playing because they don't know how much longer until the next reward. The next hole, box, or chest could be the winner. Voila, you've got an addictive game in the making.

This is just one technique used to make video games addictive. There are many more that fall under behavioral psychology. In fact, behavioral psychologists are often brought in to design products such as video games.

Though with online gaming providing real-time data about player behavior, game developers don't need psychologists' experiments with mice anymore. The gamers themselves have become the mice.

Online gaming allows developers to see which levels and missions are played longer and which are quickly abandoned. Developers analyze and dissect elements that hooked the player and include them in other aspects of the game.

This is a scary thought!

What's scarier is that this is being applied across the board to a wide array of products, services, software, and apps. There is a whole science behind it with books and courses, even at ivy league schools, teaching product developers how to make their products addictive.

As a matter of fact, *in a fall 2016 article in The Economist, Ian Leslie discusses how it is emerging as an applied discipline deployed by businesses and governments to influence the choices you make every day: what you buy, who you talk to, what you do at work. Many have made themselves wealthy as a result of applying it.*

She further writes, *the emails that induce you to buy right away, the apps and games that rivet your attention, the online forms that nudge you towards one decision over another: all are designed to hack the human brain and capitalise on its instincts, quirks and flaws. The techniques they use are often crude and blatantly manipulative, but they are getting steadily more refined, and, as they do so, less noticeable.*

What's more, humans can also get addicted to emotions. Emotions are nothing more than a complex set of chemicals released by the brain. Chemical combinations that create emotions like dopamine, serotonin, glutamate, endorphins, and norepinephrine are no different in terms of addictiveness than chemicals in drugs like caffeine, nicotine, cocaine, or even heroin. Just as the body can get addicted to chemicals in drugs and alcohol, it can become addicted to the chemicals in emotions.

To explain differently, the cells in the body have billions of receptors. These receptors are designed to accept various neuropeptides or chemicals released by the brain. There are neuropeptides for all the different emotions we feel.

Now, imagine encountering a situation that triggers the brain to release neuropeptides for fear. These neuropeptides make their way to cells and dock on the receptors. This is what causes the physical manifestation of fear. As the fear goes away, these neuropeptides release from the receptors and get flushed out of the body.

Interestingly, these are the same receptors that accept chemicals in caffeine, energy drinks, and cocaine. Like chemicals in caffeine, energy drink, or cocaine, the more these receptors are used, the more worn out and damaged they become. So, the body creates more receptors for that neuropeptide. Suddenly there is an abundance of fear receptors looking for neuropeptides for fear, and thus addiction begins.

In other words, your emotional state is a complex chemical reaction, and if the chemicals for a certain emotion are released enough, the receptors crave them more. Over time, those receptors become addicted to the emotion like they would a drug.

This might shed light on why your chronically negative spouse or persistently angry grandfather are so chronically negative or angry. They are, in some way, addicted to the chemicals of negativity and anger.

The dangers of being addicted to an emotion is that the addictive chemical is produced inside the body, so it's not something you can walk away from. When the body needs a fix, it manipulates the mind to give it the hit it needs.

In fact, the body is quite devious in how the manipulation happens. Have you ever had a carving for chocolate or sushi? Well, we often crave foods because they contain a vitamin or nutrient the body lacks or needs. If low on sugar, the body will crave sweets like chocolate. With an out of the ordinary craving like sushi, there is likely a protein the body is missing.

To fulfill the deficiency, the body persuades the mind to produce a craving. Next thing you know, you are making dinner plans with friends. What this means is when you have an addiction, the body manipulates you, your mind, and circumstances to fulfill the addiction.

How do you feel when you don't finish a task on time? Do you get down, upset, or frustrated with yourself? Well, you might be addicted to the chemicals in those emotions. If that's the case, your body will make it difficult to concentrate and get anything done, so it's receptors can get a *hit* of the neuropeptides for frustration.

If you often wait until the last minute to start a project, you might be addicted to the chemicals of stress that are released when the clock is running out. That means, your body will orchestrate behaviors so you wait until the last minute, when things are more hectic and stressful, just so it can get that rush of stress. This explains behaviors such as procrastination on a much deeper, biological level.

Since a person can become addicted to emotions, he or she can become addicted to anything. Bickering with a spouse, getting worked up with kids, or disliking a job can all become addictions. A possible reason why you haven't left the job you hate is likely because you are addicted to the chemicals of anxiety or frustration the job brings. In fact, the addiction to games, apps, news, products do not necessarily arise from the game or app itself, but the emotions released by engaging with them.

More importantly, you can become addicted to a routine. If you read the paper every morning, and have for years, you've unknowingly become addicted to it. If one morning you don't have a chance to read the paper, you'll likely experience some sort of withdrawal, making it difficult to start the day on the right foot.

In reality, habits are nothing more than addictions. They are an addiction to a behavior, routine, way of thinking, and of course, a way of feeling. The chemicals that are released to carry out an action or behavior is what creates habits. This sheds light on why habits are so difficult to break. In effect, breaking habits is the equivalent to overcoming addiction.

All this might be a lot to take in–emotions, addictions, habits. Nevertheless, it begs the question, *why would my body do something so destructive?* You must remember—the mind and body are complex systems and no system is perfect. Every system has flaws. As amazing as the body is, and all the wonderful things it does, it has its flaws.

One is that it can become addicted to the chemicals of emotions. In some respects, those addictions are good because they create habits and routines. However, when the habit or routine is no longer useful, they become unhealthy and destructive.

I admit, this is a lengthy discussion on addiction, though the purpose is to help you realize the enormous impact addictions have on concentration. As asserted, anytime a fix arises, it becomes increasingly difficult to think, make decisions, or process new information. The mind becomes so consumed on the fix, it is unable to focus on anything else.

The purpose is also to help you understand that many of your concentration issues arise from the many addictions in your life to which you may not be aware, like coffee, television, stress, and routines. These addictions are constantly disrupting focus to have the craving met.

In fact, how long you can focus is determined by your addictions. Your focus can last only until the next craving, whether that craving is for the next cat video or social media post.

As with overcoming any addiction, the first step is to admit the problem. That doesn't mean admitting that you are some sort of an addict (though by design, we are all addicts) or a person with no self-control. What it does mean is to realize that there are many parts of you affected by addiction. If left unaware, those parts can have a significant impact on concentration.

Next, realize if you are chasing the same diversion over and over, caught in the same pattern of behavior, falling back into the same routine, procrastinating with the same distractions, and always dealing with the same issues, you are likely addicted to the diversion, behavior, routine, distraction, and issue.

In those moments when concentration breaks, notice how you convince yourself to stay in the diversion, behavior, routine, distraction, and issue. *One more game won't hurt, I'll just read one more article, I'm going to reply to just one more message* are all statements addicts use to stay in addictions. When they say it, they are convinced it will only be *one* more, but the mind simply leads them to think that so they continue the behavior.

It's the most unassuming, yet deceptive trick of your mind. So, be alert for how your mind talks you into staying in addictive patterns that pull you away from more important priorities. Anytime you say one more, realize it may not be one more. That *one more* may lead to other *one mores* until you're at the point of no return.

Unfortunately, resisting addictions is not easy. It's not simply a matter of choosing to stop engaging in the addictive behavior. It takes immense awareness, intention, and will to move past.

The best and simplest advice I can offer to break an addictive pattern is to immediately stop the pattern anytime you tell yourself *one more*. Anytime you catch yourself saying one more, stop the behavior and move on to something else. If you can ingrain this into your muscles and being, you'll have an edge over any addiction that has the potential to break concentration.

This concludes the section on distractions. In this section, you learned two types of distractions–external and internal. The best ways to address external distractions are either to **remove** or **ignore** them. Internal distractions are more complex because the human mind and body are complex. Four of the more disruptive types of internal distractions come from physical pain, emotional pain, unfulfilled wants, and addictions.

You probably never thought there was so much to distractions. That might explain why you've been so easily seduced by them, even thinking you made the conscious choice to follow a distraction. The reality is, you were in one way or another manipulated by the craftiness of the internal mechanisms and outside world. Now that you're aware of their manipulative tricks, you will not be lured so easily.

SECTION V –
LIFESTYLE, ROUTINE,
AND ENVIRONMENT

CHAPTER 26 - LIFESTYLE

You've reached the last section of the book. You've learned a great deal about the inner workings of the mind and body, and no doubt, there is more to us than meets the eye. Profound reasons exist for why you do or don't do something, or why you can't get things done beyond laziness and lack of motivation. Technically, even laziness has complex motives.

Now that you have deeper insight into the inner systems at play, let's look at ways to care for and support those systems. All systems require maintenance, support, and operate better under certain conditions over others.

Think about a car—regardless of the number of features, cylinders, or horsepower it has, putting in the wrong type of oil, not enough oil, low quality oil, or even dirty oil will drastically reduce its performance. The same occurs if the car is overworked for hours on end or driven in rough roads, conditions, and environments. Even if it has luxury features, the result will be sub-compact performance.

The same applies with the systems of your mind and body. You might not be the smartest or most gifted person (just yet), but you can operate beyond the most gifted in class by giving your systems the proper care and maintenance. On the other hand, you may be the smartest and most gifted, but by not taking care of yourself, are operating far below your potential, or possibly, not at all.

This section discusses how to keep the systems of the mind and body operating at its best. It addresses 3 keys to performance, which include lifestyle, routine, and environment. This chapter will begin the discussion with lifestyle, dealing with the essential ingredients to life—sleep, diet, and exercise.

Sleep

Importance of sleep can't be overemphasized. Sleep is not only about giving the body rest. Although you may feel like the body is shutting down when crawling into bed, sleep is actually a time when certain processes get busy.

You may not realize, but while awake, the body sustains heavy damage. Tissues tear, muscles rip, and swelling occurs from activities as common as walking. Ultraviolet rays, free radicals, and other exposures harm cells, vessels, and organs. Sleep is when the body has a chance to repair these damages.

During sleep, there are less demands on the organs. For example, blood pressure drops allowing the heart to not work so hard. Having this break is vital so the organs can have the rest to function at their best the following day.

Also, while sleeping, the brain prepares for the next day. It forms new neural pathways and connections to make sense of the information you learned that day. In fact, it is during sleep that much of what we learn gets processed and integrated.

As a result, not having enough sleep can make it nearly impossible to concentrate. One sleepless night impairs performance as much as having .1 % alcohol in the blood–above the legal driving limit

On the surface, sleeping seems simple. You lie down, close your eyes, then nod off to wake up the next morning refreshed and ready. Somehow it rarely seems to happen that way. There is more to sleep than just lying down and closing your eyes. To get proper sleep, one must not only get the right amount of sleep, but go to bed at the right time.

Getting the Right Amount

The right amount of sleep is different for everyone, but on average, people need between six and nine hours to stay healthy and function properly. You can determine the right amount by trying the following experiment.

Over the course of a month, sleep for a different number of hours each week. One-week sleep for seven hours, for instance, going to bed at 10 PM and getting up at 5 AM. The next week, sleep for eight hours, and another week for six hours, and the final week for 9 hours.

Observe which quantity allows you to be up and alert, leaves you feeling tired and groggy, or like you overslept? For this experiment, go to bed the same time every night and only change the time you get up in the morning.

Sleeping at the Right Time

You will sleep better and fall asleep easier if you go to bed at the right time. That's due to the circadian rhythm, which is basically a 24-hour internal clock that is running in the background of your brain, which cycles between sleepiness and alertness at regular intervals. Have you ever noticed that you tend to feel energized and drowsy around the same time every day? That's a result of this sleep/wake cycle.

Each person's rhythm is slightly different, but for most, there is an ideal time to go to bed, usually between 9 and 11 PM. Jumping into bed too early or staying up too late can affect the rhythm, and hence, quality of sleep. Even if you are exhausted, you won't be able to doze off, or you may doze off, but not feel rested the next morning.

To discover your ideal bedtime, go to bed at different times each night. The first week, go to bed at 9 p.m. The next week, call it a night at 10:00 p.m. The following week, try 11:00 p.m. You may even experiment on the half hour–9:30, 10:30, and 11:30.

Within the optimal time, you can lie down, close your eyes, and drift off with little trouble. Outside the optimal time, you'll lay half-awake or fully awake, tossing and turning, unable to settle.

Additional Considerations

Other considerations include not watching T.V. right before bedtime, avoiding foods before bed that create indigestion, having a nighttime routine to help transition between waking and sleeping, and making sure the sleep environment is free from loud noises, bright lights, or other disruptions that can activate the distraction mechanism.

Eating Habits

Chapter 22 on Internal Distraction from Pain introduced the importance of taking in enough food and water. Though it's not just about enough food, it's also about the right food and the right time.

Concentration requires energy. In fact, it requires a lot of energy. At times, more energy than physical activity. Food supplies that energy. Not eating the right kinds of food or not eating food at the right times can leave your system with too little energy to be effective.

To properly fuel the mind and body, you want to eat foods that improve concentration, avoid those that hinder concentration, as well as to stay properly hydrated. Let's quickly dissect each of them.

Breakfast

Breakfast is a big deal—the most important meal of the day. It's a clichéé, but like many clichéés, there's an underlying truth. In the morning, the body is running a deficit. What you eat for breakfast needs to both make up for the deficit and provide enough energy to get to the next meal. Keep in mind that because the body is running a deficit, it doesn't have as much energy to digest the foods you eat.

So, for breakfast you want to go for two things: high energy and easy to digest. Good options include eggs, whole-grain hot cereal, tofu, and yogurt. It's also a good idea to tailor the quantity to the day's activities. If you are going to be physically active, spend a lot of time in the cold, which expends more energy, then eat a larger breakfast to get in more calories. This will provide the extra energy needed to sustain you through the day.

Lunch

Lunch comes as a break in the middle of the day. Depending on your perspective, lunch can be a welcome rest or an annoying distraction.

However you view this meal, it's important to stop and eat so that energy and focus remain high to the evening.

Unless you have a fast metabolism, you want to keep lunch light. A heavy lunch weighs one down, pulling blood, energy, and oxygen away from the brain. If you need to keep focus sharp after lunch, stay away from heavy carbs and dairy. Go for low-calorie, high-nutrient foods like fruits and vegetables.

Afternoon Snack

Do you have snacks in the midafternoon or do you think of them as a kid's thing, as in, arrive home from school and grab some chips? An afternoon snack should be an everyone thing. People tend to have a sudden drop in energy around mid-to-late afternoon. A small, high-energy snack like nuts, fruit, or cheese can keep energy up and concentration high. Try to snack about half an hour before you usually start feeling tired.

Dinner

For most people, dinner comes after the hard work of the day is over. So, what you eat at dinner won't necessarily affect your work for the day, that is, if you clock off before dinner. But it can affect the quality of sleep, and hence, your work the following day.

Use dinner to round out the day. If you didn't get enough protein, fruits and vegetables, or enough healthy fats during breakfast or lunch, then dinner is a good time to fill in the nutritional gaps. Also, eat dinner at least four hours before bed, and as suggested earlier, avoid anything that might cause indigestion or otherwise disturb rest.

Foods that Aid Concentrate

To keep concentration stable throughout the day, select foods with a low glycemic index. Low glycemic foods are foods that release sugars into the bloodstream slowly, over a period. This provides a steady, stable energy supply for an extended period. In contrast, high glycemic foods release their sugars quickly, leading to quick bursts of energy, which tapers off quickly, leaving a person tired and unfocused.

Foods fall into the High Glycemic Index when they are rated at 70 or above. If the Glycemic Index for a food is at 55 or lower, it is considered a Low Glycemic Index food item. Thus, Medium Glycemic Index foods are those that fall between the range of 56 to 69. Popular low glycemic foods include peanuts, pizza, apples, and spaghetti. Here is a list of options that rate low on the glycemic index.

Brown Rice	55	Macaroni	45
Apple Juice	41	Milk, fat free	32
Baked Beans	48	Milk, Soy	30
Banana	53	Oatmeal Cookies	55
Broccoli	6	Oatmeal, old fashioned	49
Carrots, cooked	39	Orange Juice, fresh	52
Cauliflower	6	Peach, fresh	28
Cheese tortellini	50	Peanuts	14
Cherries, fresh	22	Peas	48
Chocolate	49	Popcorn	55
Fruit cocktail, canned	55	Potato Chips	54
Grapefruit	25	Pound Cake	54
Grapes	43	Snickers Bar	40
Ice Cream, low fat	50	Spaghetti	41
Kidney Beans	52	Special K Cereal	54
Kiwifruit	52	Spinach	12
Lentils	28	Sweet Corn	55
Lettuce	7	Sweet Potato	54

Linguine	55	Tomato	15
Low fat Yogurt	33		

The website http://www.glycemicindex.com has a free searchable database that shows which foods have a high or low glycemic index, as well as guides on how a low glycemic diet works.

Foods to Avoid When You Need to Concentrate

There are certain foods to avoid if you're going to need concentration later. Highest on the list is sugar. While the sudden burst of energy sugar provides can seem helpful, 15 to 30 minutes later you'll crash, feeling a sudden loss of energy and concentration. Small amounts of caffeine can be helpful for keeping energy high, however, if you have too much, you'll experience a crash like that experienced from sugar. Lastly, heavy foods that sit in the stomach leave a person feeling drowsy and unable to concentrate.

Staying Hydrated

Did you know that by the time you feel thirsty, you are mildly dehydrated? What's more is that some of the first effects of dehydration interfere with motivation and concentration, causing fatigue and difficulty with tasks. Staying hydrated is crucial to keeping mental faculties in top shape.

Luckily, much of common knowledge about hydration is a myth. Non-caffeinated drinks such as juice and lemonade provide the same hydration as a cup of water. Caffeinated drinks provide less hydration than water, but still help one hydrate. On average, 1 cup of the caffeinated drink is equivalent to two thirds of the cup of water, and the mythical 8 glasses a day is exactly that—a myth.

The best way to stay hydrated is to keep a drink handy throughout the day and take sips every now and again. If you find yourself picking up a bottle of water and chugging, you're dehydrated. If you pick up that same bottle of water and feel like taking a sip or two, you're staying properly hydrated.

Alcoholic drinks, unlike caffeine, will actively dehydrate a person. Staying away from alcohol when you need to concentrate is always a good idea, but if you do indulge, say after work, make sure to drink extra water.

Physical Activity

For purposes of concentration, physical activity comes in two forms– movement and exercise. Both improve and are necessary to maintain focus, but provide benefits in different ways. The best boost to concentration requires engaging in both.

Movement

Since the body likes to move, everything from digestion to the skeletal structure, works better when in motion. This is especially true of circulation. We all know that the heart pumps blood throughout the body, but only recently did doctors realize that the heart is assisted by movement. The expansion and contraction of muscles help push blood through the veins and arteries.

When a person sits for too long, circulation slows, blood pools in the legs, and worse, less blood flows to the brain. Blood reaching the brain is crucial because blood carries oxygen and nutrients. When blood flow is restricted, the brain is less nourished, which impairs thinking, memory, and of course, focus.

There's an easy way to prevent this from happening.

Get up and move!

Every hour or so, walk to the water-cooler, check the fax, or make a copy. Pace a bit while thinking through the next steps of the project. If you are studying, walk around your desk or up and down the hallway with the study materials for a few minutes. Dance, do jumping jacks, or like a dog, shake yourself for a few seconds. Remember the advice on stretching? That's movement too. Stand up and stretch. When you return to work, you'll return focused and alert.

Movement is great for short spurts, though shortly after, circulation will gradually decline again. Therefore, make movement a regular part of your day. Take a few moments every hour or two to get the body up and in motion.

You can weave movement into breaktime. Remember, during breaks, you want to switch between mental, emotional, and physical activities. If you've been knee deep in mental and emotional activities, when stepping away, instead of switching to a similar activity or nothing at all, get up, move, and stretch. Movement combined with stretching will give you twice the boost to concentration.

Exercise

You can't throw a stick these days without it landing on some article or report advocating the health benefits of exercise. What you may not often read are the mental benefits. Exercise has been linked to strong mental abilities all the way back to ancient Greece. Modern researchers have found that contrary to the dumb jock stereotype, high school students who participate in sports do better academically than their classmates.

Exercise benefits concentration two ways. First, exercise teaches restraint, self-control, and the ability to push limits, all traits that go hand-in-hand with concentration.

Second, exercise boosts metabolism. A person who exercises regularly burns calories faster than someone who doesn't. This is, of course, why exercise is good for weight loss.

But there's another side to it.

Burning calories more quickly means having more energy. The more you exercise, the higher your metabolism. The higher your metabolism, the more calories the body burns. The more calories the body burns, the more energy you have throughout the day. And more energy equates to better focus.

Walking, aerobics, weightlifting, yoga, and swimming are all effective forms of exercise, though a good program will have you up and moving for an hour at a time, at least three days a week. When starting out, work hard enough that you can feel the effort, but not so hard that you can't carry on a normal conversation.

These are the two types of physical activity–movement and exercise–and both effective and necessary. You can think of movement as an *in the moment* tool to jazz up concentration when energy and motivation are running low. Exercise is like concentration training, its benefits are realized overtime from consistent and frequent use.

This is all as it relates to lifestyle, which examined the essential ingredients to life: eating, sleeping, and physical activity. Ingredients we all know to consider, yet somehow overlook. Hopefully this chapter has given you reasons to not overlook it so much.

CHAPTER 27 - ROUTINES

How do you schedule work? Do you have a routine or simply do things as they come up? While some jobs involve repeating the same task over and over, most require performing a variety of tasks throughout the day. By scheduling tasks based on your mood, energy level, and motivation, you can channel concentration in directions that need it most.

In other words, there are times of the day when energy and focus are high, and then times when the mind seems to zone out. When planning your day, schedule tasks that need high level of concentration for periods when you have the most energy and focus. Save the items that, as the saying goes, can be done in your sleep, for those times when energy and motivation are low.

Putting together a report for a shareholders meeting, adding finishing touches to a custom order, or drafting an essay that makes or breaks the semester are all things that require high degree of concentration. When possible, schedule these assignments when you naturally have more energy and motivation—those moments when it's easy to focus and distractions aren't as, well, distracting.

Also, if you remember from the chapter on impulse control, willpower requires energy. We tend to have less energy as the day progresses, so avoid scheduling demanding tasks or those that require a high degree of willpower for when the energy to power that will is running low. Anything you hate doing or resist requires a certain degree of will to see through, so save them for times of the day you are alert, motivated, and have energy.

Another part of the routine equation involves mixing enjoyable or rejuvenating pursuits between those that are draining. If you love filing expense reports, save them for when you are tired or have lost focus. The joy derived from the activity can be enough to recharge concentration. Or if you like leading meetings, don't schedule them first thing in the morning.

Start with other priorities, so you have something to look forward. You can think of enjoyable tasks as rewards for completing those you dislike.

For the average person, peak hours are early morning, mid-morning, post-lunch, and early evening. Schedule the more difficult, least pleasurable, highly involved activities in these blocks. Plan tedious chores like filing paperwork, checking inventory, or reviewing notes around them. Then squeeze the errands you enjoy in between both to give you the necessary recharge to continue the momentum.

This way tasks and activities flow with your energy and concentration. Instead of forcing yourself to concentrate, you are simply switching to activities that match your level of motivation in the moment. When attention is high, work on demanding activities. When it tapers, switch to less demanding or easy ones. Once focus is depleted, recharge and replenish with enjoyable tasks. It helps to write everything out in the form of an action list and then schedule the activities accordingly.

Here is an example of how I use routines to ride the concentration wave. Writing is an extremely taxing and downright mentally and emotionally draining activity for me, so it helps to be completely rested and energized when I write. As soon as I get out of bed, before doing anything else, I head to my desk, turn on the computer, and begin writing. I'll write anywhere from 45 to 90 minutes.

When focus begins to decline and I'm unable to write fluidly, I switch to less demanding tasks like responding to emails, setting meetings, or making appointments. During this time, I will have gotten a good hour of writing and some errands out of the way.

When my energy and focus is completely exhausted, I will prepare and eat breakfast. I'm still engaged in an activity, but it doesn't require mental thought or emotional strain as it is something I enjoy and can do easily. After breakfast, I am refreshed, recharged, and ready to write more.

When concentration and focus wears again, I'll shower and get dressed. Showers are really refreshing for me. They have the uncanny ability to reset my mind as if I've just woken up. So, I can put in a few more hours of strong, focused attention after jumping out of the shower. In fact, sometimes, I'll go straight to my computer since my mind is fresh.

After a few more hours of work, it's time for lunch, which presents another opportunity to step away and let the brain recharge. If I've been indoors all morning, I make it a point to eat out.

After lunch, I continue the cycle through the rest of the day, being cognizant to arrange my schedule so I'm at the optimal level for that task, activity, or assignment. This ensures I have the focus I need when I need it most.

The key to routines is to tame any and all excuses that may keep you from working during peak hours. Don't check email, watch music videos, or mindlessly read internet articles in the morning or have watercooler conversations after a lunch break. Stay focused on the difficult topics, then ride the wave with the less difficult ones.

It's important to note that peak hours vary from person to person. As mentioned, peak hours for the average person surge in the morning and after lunch. That's because we are the freshest and the weight of the day hasn't brought us down in the morning and lunch replenishes the calories to refuel us for the rest of the day.

Though that is not the case for everyone. Some are groggy and cranky in the morning and don't warm up until mid-morning. Evening people wake up later, start slower, and peak in the evening. For some, afternoon is the least productive as blood is rushing to their stomach to digest lunch; thus, they tend to feel tired during this time. The point is, peak times for the average may not be the peak for you, so it's important to find your peak.

As with breaktime, routines require discipline to stick to specific tasks at specific intervals, and that you don't start the day playing candy crush. You may not be successful in the first few tries, but remain persistent until you build a rhythm.

CHAPTER 28 - ENVIRONMENT

A few years ago, I was on a walking tour in Dublin, Ireland, and after the tour, the group and I wound down the day at a local Irish pub. At the pub, I was having an interesting conversation with a woman in the group who worked for a prestigious interior design firm. She was telling me fascinating facts about the world of interior design and the level of psychology and forethought that goes into designing a space.

For example, in fast-food restaurants, lights are bright, seating usually hard and uncomfortable, and tables crammed together. This is to encourage patrons to order, eat, and quickly leave since fast food restaurants focus on volume and high turnover.

On the other hand, in a casual or fine dining restaurant, the lighting is soft and flattering to make guests feel relaxed. Furniture is comfortable and the colors are warm. This invites customers to unwind, linger, and order more food, dessert, coffee, or an extra glass of wine.

In addition to lighting and comfort, restaurants emphasize certain colors over others. Restaurants tend to use red, orange, and yellow since these colors stimulate appetite and induce hunger. Research shows that a red table cloth makes a person eat more and faster.

It's no surprise that all major restaurant chains use red, orange, or yellow in their logo. In fact, the next time you are out, notice the logos of the restaurants you pass. Every restaurant chain, without exception, has either red, orange, or yellow in their logo.

On the other hand, rarely will restaurants decorate with blue or purple, especially as the central theme, because blue and purple suppress appetite. These colors are not common in food and the brain associates such colors to foods that are rotten or spoiled.

Restaurants also employ scents as part of the experience. Many let the aroma of baked breads and wood smoke carry from the kitchen into the seating area. If venting doesn't allow such smells to disperse, they will employ artificial scents. Scents alone are known to increase sales by 300%.

Sound too plays into the interior design equation. Quiet places make customers feel like their conversation can be heard. However, high volumes annoy people. That's not usually a problem at bars where studies suggest loud music translates to more drinking. This explains why bars are excessively loud. The tempo of the music is also considered, as faster music makes people chew faster.

Interestingly, fast food restaurants in third world countries don't follow the norms in the States. McDonald's and Burger King are expensive relative to the average wage in those countries, so for people there, these restaurants are a casual dining experience. As such, fast food restaurants in those countries mimic the casual dining experience by dimming the lights and adding comfortable seats to encourage patronage.

My new friend from the tour went on to talk about other aspects of interior design. She said that rooms with high ceilings promote free and abstract thinking, while rooms with low ceilings make people more detail-orientated. Study halls are purposely cold to keep students awake and alert.

Though nowhere is the psychology of interior design more meticulously applied than in casinos. The height of ceilings, layout of tables, patterns on carpets, and sounds of machines are all engineered to promote one and only one thing, gambling.

For starters, casinos don't have clocks or windows so gamblers lose track of time. It could be 3 p.m. or 3 a.m., but you wouldn't know. The space is usually laid out in a labyrinth-like maze with tall slot machines and tables arranged randomly, making it extremely difficult to find an exit.

Not to mention, the sounds of bells ringing, slots clinging, wheels whirling, and lights flashing along with colorful patterns and designs on the carpet hypnotize gamblers into a trance like state, making them unaware of what they are doing.

Many casinos even go as far as to not have 90 degrees turns. Hallways and walkways curve instead of making hard lefts or rights. As Natasha Dow Schüll explains in her book, *Addiction By Design: Machine Gambling in Las Vegas*, right-angle turns activate the decision-making mechanism to think about what it's doing. That's not what casinos want visitors to do.

This level of foresight goes into the design of most places including malls, department stores, hotels, libraries, offices, cafes, and movie theaters. There is a specific mood or behavior establishments seek to encourage, and they spend good money to arouse that mood or behavior.

Since the environment of a place can have such an influence on our thoughts, moods, decisions, actions, and behaviors, it follows that the right environment can influence our thoughts, moods, decisions, actions, and behaviors to concentrate. The correct combination of colors, scents, sound, and space can stimulate various parts of the unconscious to keep pushing, working, and striving even if consciously we want to give up.

So how does one create such an environment? It helps to understand how and why the mind responds to cues in the environments as described. The human mind evolved to respond to certain cues a certain way. As mentioned, we respond to red, orange, or yellow by becoming hungry, which is the reason restaurant chains employ at least one of these colors in their logo. Understanding ways the mind responds to other cues, especially those that support focus, will give you a better idea of how to shape the optimal environment.

Color

Color is one of our most basic and primary triggers. It's the first thing we see when entering a space, so it's the first sense to trigger our mind. It is almost immediate. Therefore, adding certain colors to your environment can do wonders for focus. The following is a summary of what colors to use and when, and how to employ them.

Green

Green is in the center of the color spectrum, so it is viewed as a color of balance. Green is also the color of nature. Where there are trees and plants, there is usually food and water, so the brain is reassured by green.

For these reasons, green promotes security and relieves stress, allowing you to relax and think clearer. Studies show employees who work in green offices have higher job satisfaction. Studies also show hospital patients who have a window that looks out into nature heal faster.

Blue

Blue is the color of focus and learning. Research suggests that people are more productive in blue environments. The color enhances wakefulness and supports clear communication. That is because blue is the color of the sky. When the sky is blue, visibility is clear and sharp. We are not worried about finding shelter from the rain nor threats from predators.

Brown

Like green, brown has associations with earth and nature. Brown is the color of dirt and tree trunks. As mentioned, where there are trees, there is likelihood of food and water, which brings calmness and assurance.

Reds, Oranges, and Yellows

These colors are on the high end of the color spectrum, so they are intense, engaging, and even alarming. They increase heart rate and blood flow upon sight. Therefore, they are good at grabbing attention, but not necessarily creating attention, which is the reason stop signs, fire extinguishers, and taxi cabs employ these colors.

Red, orange, and yellow are great if you want to draw people's attention to something, but not the go to choice as the theme for a classroom, workspace, or office. Although they may not be the best option for a classroom or office, they are great for environments that require physical exertion, such as a gym or workout area.

Grey's and Blacks

The color of sadness and depression, these two colors are big no-no's. When the world turns grey and the night turns black, we are instinctively conditioned to draw in and prepare for hibernation or sleep. That's the opposite of focus and concentration, so avoid these colors as much as possible.

There are many ways to spice up a work space with color. To add green to an environment, add a few easy to maintain plants around your desk or room. Or sit near a window that looks out into trees or the lawn outside.

To add blue, use blue pens and markers instead of their black counterpart. Or buy office equipment with such colors, such as printers, shelves, and even computer. In fact, the shelves and printer I currently have in my room are blue. It's easy to add brown by using hardwood floors and wooden desks and tables.

There are other ways to employ these colors. Use green, blue, or brown window curtains, decorations, or even paint one of the walls such a color. You don't have to overdo it. Just add enough in your line of sight so the mind regularly sees these colors while working.

Scent

Scents have a bigger influence on behavior than most realize. Smell is the strongest of the senses, and is the only sense that directly influences the limbic system, the control center of our emotions. It bypasses other areas of the brain and taps straight into our emotions and learning, and herein lies scent's power to influence and motivate.

Scent's power to influence and motivate is the reason retailers rely so heavily on it. Walk into Lowes or Home Depot and you're hit with the scent of freshly cut wood. You may never see a single piece cut in the store, but that smell is somehow always there. It's meant to inspire us to renovate and dive into *do it yourself*.

Airlines use scent to reduce anxiety and customer experience. Shops use scents to encourage people to enter and linger longer. Department stores use different scents throughout the store. In the men's section, they'll use scents that draw men. In the women's section, scents are more pleasing to women. In the furniture section, a different scent is employed. These scents are deliberately added.

Since scents have such a power to influence the mind, it helps to employ scents that promote concentration. Now, people mistakenly assume employing scents involves choosing those that are the most pleasant and enjoyable. That's rational thinking, though it's better to employ scents that specifically induce concentration. Following is a list of some of the more common options.

Lemon

Lemon promotes concentration and has calming and clarifying properties that are helpful when you're feeling angry, anxious, or run down. Lemon also has antiviral and antibacterial properties and fights sore throats and colds by boosting the immune system and improving circulation.

Lavender

This scent has calming properties that help control emotional stress. It also has a soothing effect on the nerves and can relieve tension and depression, as well as treat headaches and migraines.

Jasmine

Like lavender, jasmine is also used to calm nerves, but this one is also commonly used as an anti-depressant because of its uplifting capabilities that produce a feeling of confidence, optimism, and revitalized energy. All great for concentration.

Rosemary

This is the perfect Monday morning pick-me-up. In addition to improving memory, rosemary has properties that fight exhaustion, headaches, and mental fatigue. It is excellent in the mornings when one needs help to get going. It can also be used topically to relieve muscular aches and pains.

There are many ways to add or change the scent of a workspace, such as with scented candles or sprays. I don't recommend these options because they often use synthetic chemicals to mimic a particular scent, and those chemicals can be harmful to the body.

A better option is to go directly to the source and use essential oils from plants and minerals that contain the pure scent of that plant or mineral. Essential oils can be found at the local health food store, alternative medicine shop, or New Age store.

Simply inhale its aroma straight from the bottle to feel immediately energized or rub a few drops on your wrists, neck, or temples for a longer-lasting effect. You can also use a diffuser to spread the scent throughout your office, cubicle, or workspace. What's great is that scents are portable. So, while you can't always be in a super productive environment, you can bring a favorite uplifting smell to such environments.

Sound

Like scent, sound too can bypass the rational mind and trigger the unconscious directly. If a sound is pleasant, we can't help but feel invigorated to focus. If not, it's like pulling teeth. Following are examples of sound with which to experiment.

Nature

Like smell and color, our mind prefers certain sounds over others, such as those from nature like waterfalls, ocean waves, rain, or trees swaying in the wind. If you live near areas that produce such sounds, open your windows to let them in.

Background

If nature doesn't do the trick, try background noise. When it is too quiet, you might not be able to work because suddenly you notice the chatter in your head. Background noise can be useful to drown out that chatter as it gives the mind something to focus on instead of bugging you.

Examples of background noise include cafeteria, coffee shop, office, or street sounds. Research suggests that moderate chatter of a bustling coffee shop-at around 70 decibels–can distract parts of the mind just enough to encourage clearer thinking.

Although you can't always be in a coffee shop or out in nature, there are numerous software and apps that mimic such sounds. Two popular and free options include myNoise and Coffitivity.

Music

Playing music in the background is another option to improve focus. The beat, rhythm, and organized patterns in music do well to engage the mind. As the saying goes, music soothes the savage soul.

It's best to listen to songs without lyrics, since the words in lyrics can be distracting. Suitable options include symphonies, piano or violin solos, jazz, ambient, certain types of electronic, and all types of instrumental.

It's also good to choose music with a tempo that matches the task. If reading or studying, play music that is soothing and relaxing. On the other hand, with physical or challenging activities, listen to something more upbeat, like Odessa, hip hop, and if you're a fan, heavy metal. Try different varieties with different activities to see what works best.

Space

Space too has a big impact on the mind and body. In a tight or cramped space, we immediately feel claustrophobic, as if the walls are closing in on us. In an open space, the mind feels less confined, so it is free to think and be creative; though it may wander more than you like.

Optimizing space also considers whether a standing desk is better than a sitting desk, the best height for a shelf so you can easily reach everything, and the best angle of a computer screen to reduce glare and eye strain. Would having a desk lamp and a set of shelves next to the desk make things easier because everything is at arm's length?

Also consider the type of work you do. As stated, high ceilings promote free and abstract thinking, while rooms with low ceilings make people more detail-orientated. If you are an accountant, you might opt for a room with a low ceiling. A writer may like a place with a high ceiling.

I realize you can't always tear down walls or raise the height of ceilings to create the perfect environment, but can rearranging the furniture make it seem more open and less confining? If not, it helps to simply move to a place that has these features. When I am in creativity mode, I visit open spaces like a hotel lobby. When I need to focus, I go into narrow spaces, like a hole in the wall caféé.

So, these are some ways environment affects the mind and body. Though we are all different, so no one advice works for everybody, in every situation. Also, it's difficult to know how an environment will affect a person until they are in it. Even more, the environment we believe to be the least effective may be the one that triggers something in our unconscious to focus.

For these reasons, I also recommend visiting various places like coffee shops, libraries, study halls, hotel lobbies, and notice in which you focus best. It's senseless to spend time, energy, and resources to create an environment only to find it doesn't produce the desired result.

Though make sure to visit varieties of each place. That is, don't head only to the local Starbucks, visit many different types of coffee shops, such as quiet ones, loud ones, busy ones, and not so busy ones.

Then observe the characteristics of the environments you focus best – color, smell, sound, lighting, decorations, and everything in between. Are the lights bright or dim, are the colors loud or soft, is the place noisy and boisterous or quiet and calm? What type of music is playing? Pay attention also to the spacing. Is there a lot of space between the tables and chairs? How high are they? What about the energy and vibe?

Once you recognize patterns in the places you focus best, include them in your environment. If all the environments where you concentrate best have plants, add a few plants around your desk. If you work best under certain lighting conditions, buy a lamp that mimics that condition. Nowadays, you can buy inexpensive LED lamps that allow you to select various colors and brightness at the flip of a switch.

If you noticed from this discussion, we are affected by environment through the 5 senses. Color affects sense of sight, scent affects sense of smell, space is more or less touch, and sound, well, affects our sense of sound. Therefore, when fine tuning your environment, it really helps to incorporate the suggestions in Chapter 20 on Removing External Distractions. You want to not only include elements that heighten focus, but remove those that reduce it.

Nevertheless, environment is not easy to change. Few people can achieve the ideal due to office rules, budget, and other constraints. Therefore, don't feel the need to change everything at once. Start small and work your way up. Every few weeks or so add or modify something to bring the space closer to the ideal. Do what you can as every bit counts, and overtime, you will have the perfect environment that puts you in the best mood to focus.

This wraps up the chapter on environment. Adding or modifying colors, scent, sound, and space can do wonders for an environment. Hope you found the content intriguing. I surely do!

Since this wraps up the chapter, it also warps up the section on lifestyle, routine, and environment. This section taught you quite a lot from sleeping, eating, physical activity, and routines to color, scents, sound, and space. Since each suggestion produces a different effect and stimulates concentration in different ways, everyone who uses them will get different results. Take your time and experiment with changes that maximize focus.

The end of this section also marks the end of this book. Let's turn our *attention* to the conclusion and bring everything to a close.

Conclusion

So….that's all I got!

It's a wild ride you've been on, diving into the complex and oh so elusive nature of the human condition.

This book covered a lot of techniques, and I mean a lot.

With so much, it can leave anyone feeling overwhelmed, or worse, wondering if it is really that necessary to apply all the ideas to get a grip on concentration.

The goal wasn't to overwhelm, but to explain the sheer complexity of the inner-workings of the mind and body. If I only provided an explanation, without any exercises or techniques, the content would not have had any impact.

Knowledge is great for learning, but to create lasting change, that knowledge must be applied. Unless there is a format to apply it, however, it simply stays as knowledge, that over time, is slowly forgotten.

I know scores of people, from all walks of life, that read, listen, watch, and attend personal development books, blogs, podcasts, channels, and seminars by some of the biggest development gurus and coaches, yet their life stays exactly the same, completely unchanged.

It's not that the content of these gurus is not good or that their advice doesn't work, it's just people don't put it to use. The main reason is that they don't have a format to apply it. They hear the advice, understand all its ins and outs, and know exactly what to do, but they don't have a bridge to carry that knowledge into action.

The exercises, tools, and suggestions in this book are designed specifically to bridge the knowledge into action. Otherwise, it becomes a list of interesting facts, that as I stated, becomes lost and forgotten overtime.

Also, the expectation is not to apply all the techniques and suggestions in one go. Different people experience difficulty for different reasons. Unless I sat down and spoke to you one-on-one, it would be impossible to know where your challenges lie. Even a one-on-one consultation may not uncover all your issues, because there are some things I will never be able to see. They can only be seen by you closing your eyes and going inward.

Given that, it's important to have a variety of options at your disposal. This way, you can find a technique that works with your specific needs. Otherwise, it's easy to feel that the problem is hopeless, which many do when the advice they receive doesn't work.

Not to mention, even for a single person, different issues arise with different activities, in different situations, and at different moments of the day. A diverse assortment of techniques were provided to address the diverse assortment of situations you might encounter.

More importantly, as you progress in your concentration journey, certain issues will only make themselves known when others are handled. For example, your main issue right now might be impulse control. Impulses pull your attention to behaviors not conducive to concentration. After getting a handle on impulses, you'll find your thoughts also race. You never noticed the thoughts racing because impulses were at the forefront of everything else in your awareness.

After the racing thoughts are handled, you realize that you easily get overwhelmed by large projects. Due to your issues with impulses and racing thoughts, taking on sizable projects never crossed your mind, so you would have never known that could easily be an issue. But with impulses and racing thoughts out of the way, this is now the challenge at hand. The great thing about this book is that it will continue to offer advice, tips, and suggestions as you and your concentration grow.

So, use this book not as a novel that you read once, but as a resource that you revisit over and over. In the book *The One Thing*, author Gary Keller talks about determining the one thing that you can do every day that will make the biggest difference, progress, and growth in your life. The concept is not restricted to the one thing that encompasses all areas of your life, but the one thing in each area. What is the one thing you can do to improve your physical health, one thing for emotional well-being, one thing for career success, and the one thing for relationships?

As it relates to your personal development and growth, make this book your *one thing*. Do the suggested exercises daily and keep the other tools and tips on top of mind. Be aware how and when your focus is led astray and what you can do to bring it back. Given that concentration is a skill that matters more than any other skill, if it's the one thing you work on daily, the benefits will trickle to every other area of your life.

Now, I'm not advising you to make this book the one thing because I wrote it. I've written 9 other books and I never suggested that readers make any of them the one thing. I'm suggesting it with this book because I believe it matters more than any other thing. I'll talk more about why, but first...

My Story

It all begins with awareness.

Interestingly enough, my earliest childhood memory goes all the way back to my first thoughts. I was around one year old, jumping on the bed with my sister, and all of a sudden, thoughts began appearing.

It freaked me out.

I wasn't sure why the thoughts were there, where they came from, and wanted nothing more than for them to leave. It felt like there was another thinking entity in my head. It's weird to be thinking about your own thinking, especially at such a young age, but that's when I became *aware*.

Since then, I've had an un-quiet mind. In addition to the thoughts, I had extreme difficulty learning, paying attention, sitting still, organizing my ideas, communicating, interacting–anything that involved the mind, I had tremendous challenges around.

When people hear that, they immediately think Attention Deficit Hyperactivity Disorder (ADHD). Though, I would be lucky if it were only ADHD. Unfortunately, it was much more than that. My emotions were raging and cycling intensely. Some days I was lethargic, with no motivation, and barely able to get out of bed. Then other days, hyper and out of control. Somedays I was happy and wanted to hug the world, and other days, raging with anger. When people hear this, they think bipolar, and I wish it was that simple too.

Whatever I was feeling, I was feeling intensely. I was often erratic, fly off the handle, and switching states constantly. I felt like I was going to spontaneously combust, but the tragedy of it was that I never did.

I was literally changing states constantly. Frequently, I'd see the dazed look on people's eyes when one of these shifts would happen. They were so confused by how one minute I was acting one way, and another, completely different. It was almost as if I turned into another person. Since our thoughts, images, and feelings define our personality, I might as well have been another person.

I believe my challenges were brought on by three main things:

1. I was naturally an absent-minded kid. Given that I had an un-quiet mind, there was so much running in my head that I didn't have control over. As a result, I would accidentally run into the walls and smash my head against things constantly. I had bandages around my head, military war victim style, at least 12 times. Then when I was around 6, I got hit by a motorcycle, smashed my forehead straight into the ground, and was knocked out. All I remember was waking up, at home, next to my mom who was worried.

2. I have a severe reaction to processed foods. I don't know what it is exactly in food, whether it is the preservatives, e-chemicals, food coloring, or additives, eating processed food was like cocaine to me. Drinking a quarter of a can of cola would keep me up all night. If I had a McDonald's sandwich, my thoughts were racing out of control.

And it wasn't just from cola or fast food, but eating anything that wasn't whole or organic would give me intense anxiety and spin my mind into oblivion. What's worse is children's food is very much processed–candies, imitation meats and drinks, ice cream, slushies, Twinkies, and a hundred varieties of chips.

Now imagine what growing up and eating that stuff daily would do to a person with such a reaction. By the time I was an adult, I was nearly insane. I was extremely intense, incredibly anxious, and immensely hyper. I would go from zero to a hundred in a matter of seconds, talking really fast, and was essentially devoid of any self-control. I mentioned, it felt like I was going to spontaneously combust and this is how I felt on a day-to-day basis.

3. To make matters worse, I grew up in a very violent household, with a very verbally and physically abusive father, mother, and older brother. At times, living at home was like being in a war zone. I had to walk on eggshells and never knew when one of them would lose it. So, there was a lot of trauma and PTSD from that experience, creating intense levels of anxiety in myself.

By the time I got into college, I had tremendous insecurity, intensity, and to a certain degree, insanity. I assumed it was just the way I was, and that was simply my lot in life. I never made the connection to the food, trauma, or other external issues and sources. I accepted the verbal abuse of the people telling me I was lazy, didn't have any self-control, and that something was wrong with me. And I've been carrying around this belief that something is wrong with me most of my life.

Sure enough, like most people struggling with a sever turmoil that they feel has no solution, I self-medicated by getting heavy into drugs. If you can imagine processed foods messing me up, I mean, drugs messed me up. It took my hyper, sensitive, emotional, raging, and out of control self to another level.

Finally, I decided to seek help. I was initially put on an anti-anxiety and an anti-depressant. In some ways it helped me focus so I could function at work. In other ways, it was making my condition worse. Later, I was put on other medications including another anti-anxiety, and this time, an anti-psychotic.

What I found was that over time the dosage of these medications needed to be upped the longer I was on them. It made me realize what a dangerous road

I was on, because at a certain point, I would need to be on meds just to be where I was before meds, and if for whatever reason the prescriptions were discontinued or I was not able to afford them, I'd be in a worse condition. So, I immediately stopped taking the meds.

Now, anybody who knows anything about anti-depressants, anti-anxiety, or anti-psychotics knows that the last thing one should do is stop these things abruptly. Since I did, I went into psychosis and lost complete control of my mind and myself. You know those cracked out, unpredictable people on the streets talking to themselves, erratic in all their behavior? Well, that was me.

The only difference was that I was aware.

I was aware of what was going on, what I was doing, how I was behaving, and how I was coming off to people. I often joke that the thing about crazy people is that they don't know they are crazy. Because I was aware, I was able to do something about it.

At the time, I only had two options. One was to shut myself out from the world. The other was to develop strong enough self-control to contain the mayhem. The combination of the two helped tremendously. I was able to contain the chaos to interact with people in short spurts and periods. When I couldn't, I isolated myself. It wasn't healthy, but it helped get through those moments.

So, the last 15 years, I've been on a journey to get a grip on this mayhem. Like most people who start on a path of healing or growth, I sought books and courses. Though much of the advice I came across was not useful for me. It's not that they didn't work, it's that they required a certain level of self-control to apply. It was the equivalent of telling an autistic child to simply relax if an environment or situation got too intense. Unless something is rewired inside, the advice is almost useless.

But I didn't give up.

I kept trying. Short of more medication and doctors, I had a mindset that no matter what, I'd try anything and everything that came my way. And I did try anything and everything–exercise, meditation, hypnosis, all different types and styles of yoga, acupuncture, massage therapy, reiki, prayer, religion, God, spiritual cleansing, and any sort of herbal, holistic, or homeopathic remedies that I came across. I even changed my diet going as far as to become vegan, gluten-free, and organic.

Then on December 2011, I left the U.S. for 6 years. It was during this stretch when I traveled to nearly 100 countries, though the journey was less of exploration than of healing. No matter where I was in the world, whatever I came across, I tried. If I walked past an alternative medicine shop or heard about an alternative healing practice, I sought it out. Whether it was teas, drops, tinctures, powders, whatever or wherever, I'd give it a shot.

I worked with shamans in the jungles of Colombia, spiritual healers in Brazil, guides in Guatemala, guru of massage therapy from South Korea. I tried weird elixirs from the witch's market in Bolivia, and even saw a crazy witchdoctor in Africa.

A part of the healing journey involved seeking out spiritual plants like ayahuasca, iboga, mushrooms, and truffles, which are powerful plants known for their mental and emotional healing properties. If I was in a country that offered such plants, I would try them. And they aren't pleasant experiences as they are extremely intense to sit through. I spent months doing some and years doing others.

Though the most help came in the way of meditation and exercises–the very same ones offered in this book. I experimented with so many different types, styles, and varieties of mental exercises from mindfulness, vipassana, releasing, and guided visualization. At times, I would spend hours and days doing nothing but these exercises. Bit-by-bit and brick-by-brick, I began to put myself back together.

Though the journey wasn't easy. It was painful. I was in a lot of pain. It wasn't the physical type like being cut or having a broken bone, but a deeper rooted emotional and mental pain that I couldn't numb myself from, not even from drugs. It was always there. As much opportunities and luxuries, I've been presented in life, I was never happy. Given the condition, it was hard to be.

During my travels, I regularly did extreme hikes that took me to high altitudes and viewpoints. I was in so much pain and so tired of the pain, I remember on numerous occasions, I would stand at the edge of some of these cliffs thinking to myself, *one more step, I can end all this misery.* For one reason or another, I never took the step. I don't know why I never did, but I didn't.

Instead, I just kept pushing and trying new and new things. There was never one thing that was key or instrumental to my healing, but everything was a stepping stone to help me get from one stage, encounter, or lesson to the next. One exercise prepared me for another. The intensity of one psychedelic gave me the strength to do a stronger. Visiting one country equipped me with knowledge to visit another, and another, and another.

And now 15 years and nearly 100 countries later, here I am, writing about the experience. I am not fully healed from the pain, and don't think I ever will be, nor do I think it's possible for anyone to remove all the pain. Though, whatever I was seeking or searching, I realized that either it doesn't exist or that I got as close to it as I ever will.

I've just given you a small summary of a much larger, laborious journey, though when I talk about the snippets of the places I've visited, the sites I've seen, the things I've done, and the people I've met, I'm constantly told that I need to write a book.

Well, this is that book.

You see, my travels weren't a journey about exploring the world, but rather the mind. It was to leap into the human psyche and understand what makes it tick. The travels simply allowed me to access resources to dive into the human condition to release the pain, trauma, and re-wire myself from the inside.

More importantly, it was to bring that knowledge to people so they can understand who they are, what makes them tick, why they do what they do, and more importantly, why they can't get themselves to do what they so desperately yearn to do, have, and be in life. This book is a distillation of what I learned in my journey, but delivered in a way to help people improve focus, attention, and concentration.

So...

Why Concentration

Every few years, a new self-help expert claims to have the key to success, achievement, and growth. One claims that it's motivation, another claims assertiveness, while some other says it's mastering emotions. Most recently, a book came out asserting that the key trait of high performers is *grit*.

Personally, I don't think it's any of these.

I believe concentration is the most important skill anyone can develop.

That's because without concentration, you can't do anything else. You can't read a book, listen to a conversation, understand a lecture, or stick with a task. The skill is essential to decision making, evaluating options, solving problems, staying on time, driving safely, and operating dangerous machinery.

As learned in the intro, concentration is also important to relationships, because if you can't pay attention to people, those interactions can only go so far. Even traits such as motivation, assertiveness, and grit require concentration to develop, refine, and apply.

So, concentration is a big driver to everything you do and affects every area of your life.

–Kurt Vonnegut Jr, American Novelist, said "The secret to success in any human endeavor is total concentration."

–Jack Nicklaus, regarded as the greatest golfer of all time, said "My ability to concentrate has been my greatest asset."

–Michael Faraday, the most influential scientist to our daily life, listed concentration as one of the five essential entrepreneurial skills for success.

–Sylvia Porter, one of the most successful writers in America said "I've learned ruthless concentration. I can write under any circumstances… street noises, loud talk, music, you name it."

–Lee Iacocca, automobile executive known for developing the Ford Mustang and reviving the Chrysler Corporation said "The ability to concentrate is everything."

As you can see, concentration is a big deal.

It's a bigger deal than you can imagine.

In fact, it's bigger than even that.

Concentration is the single most important skill you can develop. It's the skill that matters more than any other skill and is the skill that is key to developing any other skill.

In short, what's standing between you, your goals, and happiness is not the challenge of the outside world. Most activities in life aren't that hard. Sitting down to read a book is not difficult per se nor is opening a new business.

The challenge arises when dealing with the inner thoughts, images, feelings, beliefs, habits, fears, shyness, addictions, wants, and impulses. With beliefs saying you are not good enough, fear warning that something bad will happen, addictions craving the next fix, wants longing for conflicting desires, and impulses pulling you to change gears, that's when the simple act of reading a book feels like pulling teeth.

This is where the need for motivation, assertiveness, and grit become so apparent. They are needed to push through these internal blocks and resistances. Motivation is necessary to move past fears and habits, assertiveness to overcome cravings and conflicting desires, and grit to deal with everything else.

Honestly, without these internal processes, there would be no need for motivation, assertiveness, or grit. By understanding your mechanisms, how and why they work, and ways to make them work for you, the need for such and other *keys* to success become passing thoughts. Not that these *keys* are not important, but there are deeper issues at play that need to be addressed first.

So, if there is one skill that you want to put effort on in life, it's concentration. It's the reason I recommend making this book your *one thing*.

New Model of Intelligence

Since I was a kid, whether here in the States or my native country, I was constantly bombarded with messages about the value of intelligence and the importance of being smart, as if it were a rare commodity to strive for to feel worthy, respected, or to have a good life.

I'd like to pose a new model of intelligence–awareness. Just because you don't know something, doesn't mean you are dumb, it just means that you are not aware. The information is not in your awareness. And just because the information is not in awareness, doesn't mean you are precluded from ever having it in awareness.

It's simply a matter of going out and learning it, whether from books, school, coaches, seminars, or online courses. Then once that knowledge enters awareness, doesn't mean that you're smarter or more intelligent than others, it just means that you are more *aware*.

Thinking about intelligence in terms of awareness takes away this script that we must be *smart* to be successful, financially stable, or to hold a decent conversation. They have little to do with intelligence and more about focus, hard work, and awareness–of a subject, topic, problem, situation, person, or society at large.

Experts become experts not necessarily because they are more intelligent, but because they are more aware about a topic or area of expertise. They spend the necessary time in an area or field to gain awareness in that area or field. If you spent as much time, you too could gain as much expertise, maybe a little less, but possibly even more.

A person doesn't pop out of their mother's womb as an expert on a subject. It's by putting in the work to become aware. Those with strong focus don't have to put as much effort. Those whose focus is weak do. Regardless, the more effort you can put into becoming aware, the more you'll know.

Sure, some people naturally pick up things quicker than others or figure out solutions on their own. If you want to label such people intelligent or genius, I'll concede to that. Nonetheless, it's still a matter of awareness, because if you take the time to learn the subject, you can be as aware, if not more, than them. It took me over a decade to learn the contents in this book, but in a few hours or days, you are now as aware as I am.

Not everyone can have the I.Q. of Einstein, but that's okay. You don't need it! It's not required to understand or be aware of his theories. People with far less I.Q. than his have since grasped his concepts. This puts us on a more equal footing because most anyone can become aware if they put in the time, effort, and focus.

At the end of the day, it's not about how quickly you pick up a topic anyways, but what you can do with that knowledge, and that boils down to one's ability to focus. If a person has bad beliefs, is anxious, gets easily aroused, distracted at the drop of a time, or their head is so cluttered they can't think, all the intelligence in the world will not do anything for that person.

So, don't get bogged down by the word intelligence. That's a word insecure people use to feel superior to others. Unfortunately, I was one of those people who chased intelligence to feel valuable and worthy, though slowly, I am changing that. I will say, it wasn't my intelligence that led me here, rather my awareness. And not just about what to do, but *how* to be able to do it, including how to get past limiting beliefs, distracting thoughts and emotions, and erratic impulses and drives.

All of which you now have in your awareness.

Don't let past mistakes, family of origin, socio-economic status, successes, failures, limiting beliefs about your intelligence get in the way of developing stronger focus. You are aware of the tools, now it's a matter of applying them.

Thank you for reading.

I truly hope you found the information invaluable. My goal with this book was to evolve humanity. To evolve, we must first understand who we are, how we are built, what compels us to act and react in the ways we do. If you found this book shed some light, please leave a positive review where you made the purchase. My aim is to spread the word to as many people as possible and your review can help do that.

Suggested Reading

Don't forget, if you haven't downloaded the bonus ***Conquer Your Internal Resistance to Make More Money, Have Better Relationships,*** **and** *Live a Fulfilling Life*, you can still do so at MindLily.com/ir. It's a free book that supplements this material to have you learning more, in less time, and with less effort.

If you would like to explore the mind and its fascinating qualities further, I recommend reading my other books.

Self-Talk Your Way to Success

The Art & Science of Visualization: A Practical Guide for Self-Help, Self-Healing, and Improving Other Areas of Yourself

Goal Setting: Discover What You Want in Life and Achieve it Faster than You Think Possible

Speed Reading: Learn to Read a 200+ Page Book in One Hour

Memory: Simple, Easy, and Fun Ways to Improve Memory

Mind Maps: Quicker Notes, Better Memory, and Improved Learning 3.0

Mind Mapping: Improve Memory, Concentration, Communication, Organization, Creativity, and Time Management

Lightning Source UK Ltd.
Milton Keynes UK
UKHW020816130821
388805UK00011B/769

9 781090 389718